Contents

James McNair's
BREAKFAST

Photography by Patricia Brabant

Arbor House • New York

Printed in Japan

10 9 8 7 6 5 4 3 2

Library of Congress Cataloging-in-
Publication Data

McNair, James K.
  James McNair's breakfast.

  Includes index.
  1. Breakfasts. 2. Brunches. I. Title.
II. Title: Breakfast.
TX733.M33 1987 641.5'2 87-11561
ISBN 0-87795-928-5

For the special people with whom I've enjoyed countless breakfasts:

James and Lucille McNair, my parents, and Martha McNair, my sister, with memories of the braised quail breakfasts of Christmases past;

Lenny Meyer, my companion of years gone by, who taught me to enjoy coffee and eggs and introduced me to bagels, smoked salmon, and Zabar's Russian coffeecake;

and Lin Cotton, my devoted partner, with whom I make great plans over morning coffee and healthy breakfasts at The Rockpile at Lake Tahoe and The Sunshine Cottage in San Francisco.

And a hearty welcome to the world to my nephew Christopher Devereux McNair, whose birth was announced to me while I was shooting *Grillades and Grits*.

Introduction

Nutritionists advocate breakfast as the most important meal of the day. It also happens to be my favorite meal. Such was not always the case, however.

Like too many youngsters, I hated breakfast and skipped it whenever my mother allowed. Back then I'd much rather sleep late than eat, so I usually wolfed down a piece of toast or a bowl of cold cereal before making the two-block dash to school. I detested eggs in any form—probably because they were always overcooked for my taste, I later discovered. My morning meal habits only got worse during college and graduate school, where I usually downed a Coke and a package of cupcakes or doughnuts en route to class across campus. I'll never know how much more I might have gotten out of school if I'd taken time for a good breakfast.

During those formative years, there were occasional exceptions to my anti-breakfast attitude. For as long as I can remember, the traditional Christmas morning feast in our home centered around quail that my daddy killed, my mother braised, and my sister and I ate with gusto. And somehow I always managed to have plenty of time and a hearty appetite for breakfast whenever my mother cooked pancakes or waffles.

Likewise, I enjoyed breakfast whenever we went to Mississippi to visit Mamaw and Papaw Keith, Uncle Sanford, Aunt Doris, and Cousin Sandra Kay. Whether breakfast was served in their roomy kitchen by the wood cookstove in the old plantation house out from Pickins, or later in their gentrified neighborhood of Jackson, I found the thick slices of smoked ham, piping-hot white biscuits, homemade jelly, sliced Cheddar cheese, and occasional garden-ripe tomatoes worth getting up early for.

When I moved on my own to New Orleans, I discovered the pleasures of breakfasting Creole style—at any hour of the day—on hot *beignets* dusted with powdered sugar, grillades and grits, or fried rice *calas*. Recipes for all those happily remembered tastes are included in this book.

A few years later, in New York City, my taste for breakfast foods expanded greatly. My friend Lenny Meyer slowly converted me to coffee and eggs and introduced me to the pleasures of bagels, smoked salmon and whitefish, and Zabar's Russian coffeecake. While shopping in the dawning hours of the morning for flowers and plants for a retail boutique, my partners Richard Champion and Bob Springman and I planned the daily schedule over stacks of pancakes or delectable French toast in a tiny Greek coffee shop tucked into the bustling flower market. And for several years I frequently enjoyed my own version of *Breakfast at Tiffany's,* munching on take-out deli corn muffins and sipping freshly squeezed orange juice while arranging flowers for the store's table settings.

The past decade-plus of living in San Francisco and at Lake Tahoe has seen another expansion of my breakfast repertoire. Whether in retreat during my writing periods or entertaining a houseful of friends, I enjoy getting up and filling the air with the aromas of strong coffee, freshly cut fruits, and grain-rich muffins, oven-puffed pancakes, or crunchy corn pancakes filled with blueberries.

Most of us use up more energy during the morning hours and therefore need the long-lasting fuel provided by a well-balanced meal. The heaviest concentration of recipes in this book lies in the dishes made from grains, rich in the carbohydrates that leave us feeling satisfied.

I've tried to favor *complex* carbohydrates (starches) found in whole grains, which fuel our bodies with energy. We all need to downplay the *simple* carbohydrates (the sugars) with the exception of the natural sugar found in fruits. This doesn't mean giving up maple syrup on pancakes, just being judicious.

The ideal breakfast also includes adequate protein. In addition to meats, this can come from cheese, yogurt, and other dairy products; nut butters; and legumes combined with whole grains, seeds, or nuts.

Much has been said of late about the need for fiber at breakfast. A diet rich in whole grains and whole fruits is a much tastier way of getting that fiber than is ruining a good glass of juice by stirring bran or other fiber products into it.

To cut down on fats at breakfast, choose lean cuts of meat instead of bacon or sausage (enjoy these old favorites only on special occasions); steam, poach, or bake meats instead of frying; use nonstick cookware that requires little or no fat; coat pans with vegetable-oil spray instead of using butter or oil; use skimmed or low-fat dairy products; substitute yogurt for sour cream; use butter in moderation or blend it with part safflower or other high-polyunsaturated margarine, or choose a reduced-fat brand of spread (avoid spreads that use unhealthy hydrogenated oils).

Except for baked goods, to which salt cannot be added after cooking, I've not specified amounts of salt since most of us have drastically cut back on its use. Even in the baked goods, the salt can be eliminated without sacrificing the end results. Salt according to your own needs, tastes, and doctor's advice.

Most of the recipes in this collection emphasize good nutrition. There are, however, scattered recipes for dishes rich in fats and sweeteners for those special occasions when indulgence seems justified. I certainly don't advocate eating this way day after day, but we can enjoy those dishes from time to time as long as our standard breakfasts emphasize foods that are low in fat, adequate in protein, and high in complex carbohydrates. The key to good nutrition at any time of the day is a well-balanced diet that includes a wide variety of foods—not the same English muffin and fried egg or bowl of granola day after day.

But I find breakfast to be much more than just the main energizing meal of the day. Through the years the morning meal has provided me with some of life's most pleasurable moments. Whether it's Mimosas and Puffed Oven-Baked Pancakes at a table set with crisp linens, my best dishes, and fresh flowers for a cheerful celebration with friends, or a solitary Caffè Latte and a Fresh Apple Muffin in a peaceful nook, a relaxed breakfast sets the tone for a happy and productive day. May this book add pleasure to your mornings.

BEVERAGES & FRUITS

Coffee

Coffee flavor and strength is a matter of taste. Beans from the various coffee-growing regions of the world produce different flavors. The type of roasting determines the darkness and intensity of flavor; French or Italian roasts are the most intense. Whether regular or decaffeinated, and whatever the bean or the roast, be sure the coffee is absolutely fresh by buying from a reliable dealer. Purchase only as much as you can use in a few days' time. For maximum flavor buy whole beans, store them in a tightly closed container in the refrigerator or freezer, and grind only as much as you need for each pot. Consult the coffee equipment manufacturer's directions for the correct grind.

As a general rule, use 1 standard coffee scoop (2 level tablespoons) of freshly ground regular or decaffeinated coffee to each cup of water. Adjust this measurement to your taste.

I prefer making coffee in one of two ways. If the brew will be used immediately, I often use a plunger system pot. Place the coffee grounds in the bottom of the clear glass beaker fitted inside a metal or plastic frame. Add water that's been brought just to a boil and let it stand for about 5 minutes before plunging down the tightly fitting mesh filter, which traps the grounds in the bottom of the pot.

When planning to sip longer, I prefer to drip the coffee through a paper filter into an insulated pot that will keep the drink hot for several hours without further heating, which destroys the flavor. Set the filter in the plastic cone that fits on top of the plastic pot, add the freshly ground coffee, pour water that's been brought just to a boil over the grounds, remove the cone after the coffee has dripped, and screw on the tightly fitting cap.

If you choose to make coffee in an electric drip pot, be sure to make only enough to be used within a few minutes. Otherwise the coffee will burn from sitting on the heating element. To save the flavor for longer keeping, pour the freshly dripped coffee directly into a heated insulated pot. Avoid percolators or other pots that use too high a heat and boil—thus ruin—good coffee.

No matter what type of coffee maker you choose, be sure it is immaculately clean before brewing. Coffee leaves an oily film inside the pot that can taint the flavor of fresh coffee.

Milk added to coffee helps neutralize the acid in the brew and provides some nutrition. I always heat milk in a saucepan or in a pitcher in the microwave, both to enhance the milk's flavor and to avoid cooling the coffee.

ESPRESSO is made from dark, double-roasted beans that are ground to a fine powder. Authentic espresso can be made only in an electric or stove-top espresso maker in which water is forced by high pressure through the coffee. Use 2 level tablespoons espresso to 3/4 cup water. Follow the espresso maker manufacturer's instructions. Add a twist of lemon peel if desired, and sweetener to taste.

CAPPUCCINO is espresso coffee topped with the thick foam that results from steaming milk in a machine that has a spigot for steaming. Make espresso in a large cup, follow the manufacturer's instructions for steaming the milk, spoon the resulting foam onto the top of the coffee, and sprinkle with cinnamon or powdered sweet chocolate if desired. Add sweetener to taste.

CAFFÈ LATTE combines espresso with steamed milk, topped off with the foam from steaming. Pour espresso into a mug or heat-resistant glass, pour in the steamed milk to taste, usually in equal portions, sprinkle with cinnamon or sweetened grated chocolate if desired, and add sugar to taste.

CAFÉ AU LAIT combines strong dark-roast coffee with milk that's heated to just under the boiling point. Make a pot of coffee, heat milk in a saucepan, and pour the two into a cup or mug to taste, usually in equal portions.

Black Tea

A perfect pot of tea starts with good-quality loose tea. While you are bringing a kettle of freshly drawn cold water just to a boil, warm a clean nonmetal teapot with hot water, then drain. Place 1 teaspoon of tea leaves in the pot for each cup of water you will add, plus a traditional extra one "for the pot." Pour the boiling water over the tea leaves and steep for 3 to 5 minutes; cover the pot with a quilted or insulated tea cozy to keep the tea hot. Fill a second teapot with boiling water for adjusting the strength of the brew in the cup. Stir the tea once to distribute the flavor and pour through a strainer into teacups or glasses. Add a sweetener, milk, or lemon if you wish.

To prepare hot-weather iced tea, pour boiling water over the tea leaves and steep until very strong, about 15 minutes. Pour into a pitcher and add cold water to the desired strength. Serve over ice with fresh mint, lemon or orange slices or juice, and a sweetener if desired.

VARIATIONS: Mix into any dry tea leaves some dried or fresh herb leaves, pesticide-free rose or other fragrant flower petals, bits of lemon or orange peel, pieces of vanilla bean, or whole spices such as cloves or pieces of cinnamon stick. Blend well and store in an airtight container.

Herbal Tea

Keep in mind that herbal beverages are made from the same plant parts as many medicines; in some people they can cause as many problems as the caffeine of coffee or black tea may cause, so use judiciously.

Drinks made from the leaves of one kind of herb or a mixture of herbs are made by *infusion,* or steeping in hot water. Bring freshly drawn cold water to a boil. Meanwhile, warm a clean nonmetal teapot with hot water, then drain. For each cup of water, place 2 to 3 teaspoons fresh herb leaves, or 1 to 2 teaspoons dried herb leaves, in the pot. Cover with the boiling water and steep from 5 to 10 minutes, covering the pot with a tea cozy to keep the brew warm. Strain into cups and add sweeteners or lemon if you wish.

Drinks made from seeds, roots, or bark are made by *decoction,* or boiling in water, to bring out the flavor. Place the plant part in a pot of water, following the proportions for leaves. Bring to a boil over medium-high heat, reduce the heat to medium, and gently boil for 15 to 20 minutes. Strain into cups and add sweeteners or lemon to taste.

Hot Mulled Cider

Great on frosty mornings—especially with *Beignets* (page 60) or warm muffins.

6 cups apple or cherry cider
1/4 cup packed brown sugar, or to taste
1 3-inch cinnamon stick
5 or 6 whole cloves
5 or 6 whole allspice
Zest of 1 lemon or orange, cut into julienne

Combine all ingredients in a saucepan over medium heat, stirring until the sugar dissolves. Bring just to the boiling point, then reduce the heat to low, cover, and simmer to blend the flavors, about 10 minutes. Strain and serve.

Serves 6.

French Hot Chocolate

Reserve this rich cup for those special mornings of overindulgence.

2 ounces (2 squares) unsweetened baking chocolate,
    broken or chopped
3 ounces (3 squares) bittersweet or semisweet
    chocolate, broken or chopped
1/2 cup granulated sugar
2 1/2 cups milk
2 cups light cream (or half-and-half) or
    heavy (whipping) cream
3/4 teaspoon vanilla extract

Combine the chocolates, sugar, milk, and cream in a saucepan over medium heat. Stir frequently with a wire whisk or wooden spoon until the chocolate melts and the sugar dissolves. Heat until just under the boiling point. Remove from the heat and beat in a blender or with a rotary beater until smooth and frothy. Add the vanilla and serve hot.

Serves 4.

Mexican Hot Cocoa

This spicy hot drink is popular throughout Mexico.

1/4 cup powdered unsweetened cocoa
1/4 cup packed brown sugar
1 cup water
1 3-inch cinnamon stick
3 or 4 whole cloves
Salt
3 cups low-fat milk
3 teaspoons vanilla extract
Cinnamon sticks for stirring (optional)

Combine the cocoa, brown sugar, water, cinnamon stick, cloves, and a pinch of salt in a saucepan over medium heat. Bring to a boil, reduce the heat to low, and simmer for about 5 minutes.

Stirring constantly with a wire whisk or wooden spoon, add the milk to the hot cocoa. Bring to just below the boiling point. Remove from the heat and stir in the vanilla. Strain to remove the cinnamon stick and cloves. Beat in a blender or with a rotary beater until foamy. Serve piping hot, with cinnamon sticks for stirring if desired.

Serves 4.

Berry Refresher

Add this change-of-pace juice to your summer breakfast table.

4 cups fresh strawberries, hulled, or raspberries, or a combination
2 cups freshly squeezed apple or orange juice
1/4 cup freshly squeezed lemon or lime juice
Granulated sugar
Fresh mint for garnish

Combine the berries and juices in a blender and mix until very smooth. Add sugar to taste, and strain if you wish. Chill, or serve over a little crushed ice. Garnish each glass with a sprig of mint.

Serves 4.

Sparkling Citrus Blend

Although nutritionally it's better to eat the whole fruit, most of us love morning juices, especially freshly squeezed. They can, however, be a shock to the system, and most nutritionists advise diluting the juice; I enjoy adding sparkling water to freshly extracted juice. In this refreshing blend, the mixed juices can be held covered in the refrigerator for a short time before serving. Stir in the sparkling water or wine at the last minute.

3 cups freshly squeezed orange juice
1 cup freshly squeezed pink grapefruit juice
1/4 cup freshly squeezed lemon juice
About 2 cups sparkling water or sparkling wine
Slices or wedges of one of the fruits for garnish

Combine the juices in a blender and mix until well blended. Quickly stir in the sparkling water, garnish with fresh fruit, and serve immediately.

Serves 4.

Bellini

Harry's Bar in Venice introduced this sparkling eye-opener. Make your own peach nectar, preferably from white varieties such as Babcock or Springtime, by puréeing, then straining the fruit.

2 cups fresh or canned white peach nectar
1 bottle (750 ml) Asti spumante or other dry sparkling wine, chilled

Distribute the nectar equally among 4 fluted glasses. Slowly add the Asti spumante to fill the glasses, mix gently, and serve immediately.

Serves 4.

Mimosa

This old favorite always adds sparkle to any special breakfast.

2 cups freshly squeezed orange juice
1 bottle (750 ml) brut champagne or other dry sparkling wine, chilled
Fresh mint leaves or borage flowers for garnish

Distribute the orange juice equally among 4 champagne glasses. Slowly add champagne to fill the glasses, mix gently, garnish with mint or borage, and serve immediately.

Serves 4.

Bloody Mary

3 cups chilled tomato juice
1/3 cup freshly squeezed lemon juice
1 tablespoon prepared horseradish
1 1/2 teaspoons Worcestershire sauce, or to taste
Salt
Freshly ground black pepper
Tabasco sauce
1 cup chilled vodka, aquavit, or tequila
Fresh basil sprigs or inner celery stalks with leaves
    for garnish

Combine the tomato juice, lemon juice, horseradish, Worcestershire sauce, and salt, pepper, and Tabasco to taste in a blender and mix thoroughly. Stir in the vodka and pour into 4 ice-filled glasses. Garnish with basil or celery.

Serves 4.

Ramos Fizz

Tradition has it that this drink was invented in New Orleans in the 1880s. This is my photographer's nontraditional, tastier version.

3/4 cup gin
3/4 cup sweet-and-sour drink mixer
1 1/2 cups light cream (or half-and-half) or
    heavy (whipping) cream
6 tablespoons orange curaçao or triple sec
Juice of 1/2 lime
4 egg whites
1 cup crushed ice
Powdered sugar
Freshly grated nutmeg

Combine all ingredients, including powdered sugar and nutmeg to taste, in a blender and blend until thick. Divide equally among 4 tall chilled glasses.

Serves 4.

Yogurt Smoothy

Nutritious breakfasts-in-a-glass are good alternatives for those hurried mornings.

1 cup plain low-fat yogurt
1 cup crushed ice
2 cups chopped fresh fruit, one kind or a combination
Sugar
Vanilla or almond extract (optional)

Combine all ingredients in a blender and purée until smooth.

Serves 2.

Breakfast Bahia

My friend Lenny Meyer and I often enjoyed this quick liquid breakfast during our hectic years in New York City.

1 cup milk
2/3 cup orange juice, preferably freshly squeezed
2/3 cup pineapple juice
1/3 cup cream of coconut (available wherever drink
    mixers are sold)
1/2 teaspoon coconut extract
1 banana
2 eggs
3 ice cubes
Fresh pineapple for garnish

Combine all ingredients except the fresh pineapple in a blender and blend until liquefied, about 10 seconds. Serve immediately in frosted glasses. Garnish with fresh pineapple.

Serves 2.

Fresh Fruits

Whether served alone, mixed together in seasonal compotes, or artfully combined on individual plates, luscious fruit is one of the most welcome pleasures of any morning meal. For optimal flavor, always choose whatever is in its natural season—not forced to meet supermarket demands. Ripen the fruit to perfection before serving it chilled or at room temperature, according to your preference. When combining, choose compatible fruits. (I have a prejudice against mixing crisp apples with soft fruits and prefer using them on their own.) Here are a few ideas to stimulate your imagination.

Slice bananas, preferably red or other stubby varieties, into individual bowls and top with lightly sweetened heavy cream; sprinkle with toasted nuts for a change of pace.

Serve whole, quartered, or sliced figs with lightly sweetened cream; peel green figs, leave black types intact.

Marinate mixed soft fruits or mixed citrus in freshly squeezed orange juice; garnish with fresh pomegranate seeds when in season.

Generously sprinkle mixed melon balls or cubes with chopped fresh mint and add a splash of champagne just before serving.

Combine several types of summer berries and serve with a dollop of crème fraîche, plain or vanilla yogurt, or a berry sorbet.

Combine tropical fruits (papaya, pineapple, mango, bananas, or some of the newly available exotics), add a splash of rum or pineapple juice, and sprinkle with freshly grated coconut and/or minced crystallized ginger.

Stand thin slices of peeled cantaloupe or other melon (except watermelon) upright in a basket or bowl and fill the center with fresh berries.

place in the refrigerator to soften for about 1 hour before serving.

Serves 6.

VEGETABLE VARIATIONS: Substitute 4 cups puréed vegetables (peeled ripe tomatoes, peeled cucumbers, cooked beets or carrots) or vegetable juice for the fruit. Season to taste with salt and pepper. Stir in about 1 cup plain low-fat yogurt if desired; freeze and serve as above, garnished with fresh herbs.

Apple Butter

You can also use this technique with blueberries, pears, nectarines, peaches, plums, or strawberries. I prefer the intense taste of the fruit alone, but you may choose to add cinnamon and cloves to taste when you add the sweetener.

8 tart apples (about 2 pounds), cored and coarsely chopped
1 cup unfiltered apple juice or cider
About 1 2/3 cups packed brown sugar or honey
Grated zest and juice of 1 lemon

Combine the apples and the juice in a heavy saucepan over medium heat and cook until the fruit is soft and the liquid has evaporated, about 10 minutes. Purée in a food processor or blender, or put through a food mill or strainer. Measure the purée into a heavy saucepan and add about 1/3 cup brown sugar or honey, or to taste, for each cup of apple purée. Cook over *very* low heat, stirring occasionally, until very thick and dark brown, from 2 to 4 hours.

Store in the refrigerator for up to a week, or pour into hot sterilized jars and seal tightly.

Makes about 5 cups.

Morning Sorbets

Instead of juice, begin a hot-weather morning with a slushy fruit concoction that's eaten with a spoon. Purée the fruits in a food processor or blender.

1 cup granulated sugar
1 cup water
4 cups puréed fresh berries or melon;
    or puréed poached nectarines, peaches, or pears;
    or freshly squeezed juice
Fresh mint leaves or edible flowers for garnish

Combine the sugar and water in a saucepan over high heat and boil until the sugar dissolves. Remove from the heat and cool, then add to taste to the puréed fruit. Freeze in an ice cream maker or sorbet machine according to the manufacturer's directions. Garnish and serve immediately, or store in the freezer, then

Egyptian Spiced Fruits (Koschaf)

Serve in bowls, with plenty of the spicy poaching syrup.

1 1/2 cups dried figs, preferably white, stems removed
1 1/2 cups pitted prunes
1 1/2 cups dried apricots, nectarines, or pears,
        preferably unsulphured
3/4 cup golden raisins
1 lemon, preferably Meyer variety, thinly sliced,
        then cut into half circles
2 3-inch cinnamon sticks
1/2 cup granulated sugar, or to taste
1/2 cup pine nuts
1/3 cup freshly squeezed lemon juice
Heavy (whipping) cream for passing (optional)

Place the figs in a large saucepan and cover with warm water. Soak for 1 hour, then drain. Add enough fresh water to cover the figs by 3 inches, place over medium heat, and simmer until just soft, 5 to 10 minutes. Add the prunes, apricots, raisins, sliced lemon, cinnamon sticks, and sugar. Simmer over low heat, stirring gently, until the sugar dissolves, about 5 minutes. Remove from the heat. Add the pine nuts, lemon juice, and enough water to cover the fruit by 3 inches. Refrigerate, covered, for several days to allow the fruits to absorb the liquid and develop flavor.

Serve chilled, at room temperature, or warmed. Pass the cream for drizzling over the top if desired.

Serves 8.

Baked Stuffed Apples

Select good baking apples such as Rome or Golden Delicious.

4 large baking apples
3 tablespoons dried currants or raisins
2 tablespoons light brown sugar
2 tablespoons unsalted butter, melted
2 teaspoons freshly squeezed lemon juice
1 teaspoon ground cinnamon
1/4 cup Granola (page 22)
1/2 cup apple juice
Heavy (whipping) cream or light cream
        (or half-and-half)

Preheat the oven to 350° F.

Core the apples, being careful not to go all the way through to the bottom, and remove about 1/2 inch of the peel around the top of each apple. Trim the bottom if necessary to stand the apple upright, and place the apples in a small baking dish.

Combine the currants, 1 tablespoon of the brown sugar, 1 tablespoon of the melted butter, the lemon juice, and the cinnamon in a bowl. Stir well, and then spoon the filling equally into the hollowed cores of the apples. Sprinkle the tops of the cored apples with the granola.

In a small bowl, combine the apple juice with the remaining 1 tablespoon brown sugar and 1 tablespoon melted butter. Blend well. Pour the mixture over the tops of the apples. Cover the apples with a lid or foil and bake for 30 minutes. Remove the cover and bake, basting frequently with the pan juices, until the apples are tender when pierced, about 30 minutes longer. Serve warm or at room temperature. Pass a pitcher of cream to pour over the apples at the table.

Serves 4.

Fig Preserves

Among my fondest childhood memories are the hours spent in a fig tree across the levee from the Baptist parsonage where I lived. Even though the river has since claimed that tree, the fig preserves that my mother makes and sends me every year whisk me back to those carefree days. I never get enough. Our family friend, "Miss Carrie" Smith, who lived to be almost a hundred, first showed us how to make these delectables.

Ripe fresh figs
Granulated sugar

Peel the figs carefully, removing as little pulp as possible and retaining their natural shape. Measure the figs and place them in one layer in the bottom of a heavy pot. Pour on an equal measure of sugar. Add about 1 cup water for every 2 cups of figs and shake the pot until the figs are covered with sugar. Place over very low heat and cook until the sugar melts. Increase the heat to medium and cook just until the figs are clear and the liquid bubbles to a thick syrupy consistency, about 45 to 55 minutes. Remove from the heat, cover the pot, and let stand overnight at room temperature.

Store in the refrigerator for up to a week, or reheat the figs, pack into hot sterilized jars, and seal tightly.

Lemon Curd

This tangy spread does wonderful things to warm muffins and grain-rich loaf breads such as the Oatmeal Loaf on page 28. Add grated lemon zest for a stronger lemon flavor.

3 cups granulated sugar
3 eggs
Juice of 3 lemons
5 tablespoons unsalted butter

Place the sugar in a mixing bowl and add the eggs, one at a time, beating well after each addition. Stir in the lemon juice, then pour the mixture into the top pan of a double boiler set over simmering water. Add the butter, 1 tablespoon at a time, stirring constantly until the butter melts. When the mixture is thick enough to coat a metal spoon, remove from the heat and cool completely before using. Keeps in the refrigerator for several weeks.

Makes about 2 cups.

Berry Butter

During berry season, stir up this quick treat to spread on muffins, toast, or pancakes. In other seasons, use frozen berries.

1/2 cup (1 stick) unsalted butter, softened
1/4 cup powdered sugar
1 cup fresh raspberries or strawberries, hulled,
    or thawed and drained frozen berries

Combine the butter and sugar in a food processor or blender and blend until smooth. Add the berries and run until blended. Chill until shortly before serving. Can be stored in the refrigerator for about a week.

Makes about 1 cup.

GRAINS

Granola

Most commercial granolas are coated with oil or butter and heavily sweetened with honey. Try this version for a reduced-calorie, high-energy breakfast or snack. Store in tightly sealed plastic bags or glass jars in a cool place.

2 1/2 cups regular (not instant) rolled oats
2 tablespoons whole wheat flour
3 tablespoons nonfat dry milk
1/3 cup sesame seeds
1/2 cup sunflower seeds
1/2 cup chopped almonds
2 teaspoons grated lemon or orange zest
1 tablespoon ground cinnamon
1/3 cup frozen unsweetened apple juice concentrate,
     thawed
1/2 cup hot water
1/2 cup chopped dates or granulated date sugar
     (available in natural-foods stores)
1/2 cup dried currants

Preheat the oven to 300° F.

In a large mixing bowl, combine the oats, flour, dry milk, sesame and sunflower seeds, almonds, lemon or orange zest, and ground cinnamon. Mix well. Add the apple juice concentrate and hot water and mix thoroughly.

Thinly spread the mixture in shallow baking pans and bake until dry and toasted, stirring occasionally, about 40 to 45 minutes. Pour into a large mixing bowl and cool slightly before stirring in the chopped dates and the currants. Cool completely before storing.

Makes about 5 cups.

Swiss Cold Oat Cereal

1 1/3 cups regular (not instant) rolled oats
2 cups freshly squeezed orange juice or water
2 teaspoons freshly squeezed lemon juice
3/4 cup chopped almonds
2 apples, grated, or 2 cups fresh berries,
     sliced fresh fruits, or reconstituted dried fruits
Toasted pumpkin or sunflower seeds (optional)
Plain low-fat yogurt, milk, or cream
Honey, date sugar, or other sugar

Combine the oats and orange juice in a bowl, cover, refrigerate, and leave overnight.

Just before serving, stir in the lemon juice, almonds, apples or other fruit, and seeds. Spoon into individual serving bowls. Pass the yogurt, milk, or cream and the sweetener at the table.

Serves 4.

Hot Multi-Grain Cereal

Several brands of mixed-grain cereals are available for quickly cooking into cold-day treats. Here's how to mix up your own grains, then store them for cooking as needed. The amounts can be varied according to taste and availability. Both packaged mixed-grain cereals and the individual dried grains can be found in natural-foods stores and some supermarkets.

CEREAL MIX

1 cup dried hominy corn
1 cup triticale berries
1 cup brown rice
1 cup dried millet
1 cup barley grits (cracked barley)
1 cup steel-cut oats (Scotch oats)
1 cup dried bulgur (cracked wheat)
1 cup sesame seeds

4 cups water, milk, or apple juice
1 teaspoon salt, or to taste
Ground cinnamon (optional)
1/4 cup raisins
Brown sugar or maple syrup
Warm milk or heavy (whipping) cream

To prepare the cereal mix, place the hominy corn, triticale berries, brown rice, and millet, separately or in combination, in a food processor and pulse quickly to crack them into small pieces.

Combine all the grains with the sesame seeds in a large bowl and mix thoroughly. Store in airtight containers in a cool place or in the refrigerator.

To cook, bring the water, milk, or apple juice to a boil in a saucepan over medium-high heat. Stir in 1 cup of the mixed grains, the salt, cinnamon, and the raisins. Cook until the grains are tender, 7 to 10 minutes. Sweeten to taste with sugar or syrup and serve with warm milk or cream.

Serves 2 (cereal mix for 16).

Fruity Oatmeal

A perfect rib-sticking start for a wintry day.

2 cups water
2 cups low-fat milk
2 cups regular (not instant) rolled oats
1/2 teaspoon salt
3/4 cup chopped pitted prunes or raisins
2 apples or firm pears, shredded
Ground cinnamon
Milk, heavy (whipping) cream, or light cream
  (or half-and-half), warmed
Brown sugar or maple syrup

Combine the water, milk, oats, and salt in a heavy saucepan over medium-high heat. Bring to a boil, cover, reduce the heat to low, and simmer for 5 minutes. Stir in the prunes, apples, and cinnamon to taste. Simmer, stirring frequently, until tender, about 5 minutes more. Serve hot. Pass warmed milk or cream and the sweetener.

Serves 4.

Berry Muffins with Nutmeg Sugar

Vary blueberries and cranberries according to the season.

1 1/2 cups unbleached all-purpose flour
2 teaspoons baking powder
1/4 teaspoon salt
1 teaspoon ground cinnamon
1/2 teaspoon freshly grated nutmeg
2 eggs
1/3 cup granulated sugar
3 tablespoons maple syrup
1 cup low-fat milk
1/4 cup vegetable oil
1 1/2 cups fresh cranberries, coarsely chopped,
    or 1 1/2 cups fresh blueberries, picked over
1 tablespoon granulated sugar combined with
    1 teaspoon freshly grated nutmeg

Preheat the oven to 400° F.

Combine the flour, baking powder, salt, cinnamon, and nutmeg in a medium-sized bowl.

In a large bowl, beat the eggs. Add the sugar, syrup, milk, and oil; mix well. Add the flour mixture, stirring until ingredients are just blended. Fold in the berries. Fill greased muffin tins about two-thirds full and sprinkle the tops with the nutmeg sugar.

Bake until the muffins are lightly browned and a wooden skewer inserted in the center comes out clean, about 20 minutes. Remove immediately from tins and cool briefly on a wire rack.

Makes 12 muffins.

Bran Muffins

I never tire of these dark, moist, and nutritious delights.

1 1/2 cups unprocessed wheat or oat bran flakes,
    or a combination
1 cup dried currants or raisins
1/4 cup molasses
1/4 cup honey
1 cup low-fat buttermilk
2 eggs, lightly beaten
1/2 cup vegetable oil
1 teaspoon vanilla extract
3/4 cup unbleached all-purpose flour
1/4 cup whole wheat flour
1 1/2 teaspoons baking powder
1/2 teaspoon baking soda
1 1/2 teaspoons ground cinnamon
1/2 teaspoon freshly grated nutmeg
1/2 teaspoon ground allspice

Combine the bran flakes, currants, molasses, honey, buttermilk, eggs, oil, and vanilla extract in a large bowl. Stir well. Let stand to soften the bran, at least 20 minutes, or cover and refrigerate as long as overnight.

Preheat the oven to 425° F.

In a medium-sized bowl, combine the flours, baking powder, baking soda, cinnamon, nutmeg, and allspice, stirring to blend. Add the dry mixture to the moist bran mixture, stirring just enough to blend together. Spoon into greased muffin tins, filling about three-quarters full. Bake until browned, 15 to 20 minutes. Remove immediately from tins and cool briefly on a wire rack.

Makes 12 muffins.

Fresh Apple Muffins

1/2 cup vegetable oil
1/2 cup granulated sugar
2 eggs
1/2 teaspoon vanilla extract
1 1/2 cups unbleached all-purpose flour
1/2 cup whole wheat flour
1 tablespoon baking powder
1/2 teaspoon salt
1 1/2 cups peeled and chopped raw apples
1/2 cup chopped walnuts

Preheat the oven to 350° F.

In a large bowl, combine the oil, sugar, eggs, and vanilla; beat with an electric mixer or wire whisk until creamy smooth.

In a separate bowl, combine the flours, baking powder, and salt. Add to the egg mixture, beating just until well blended. Fold in the apples and nuts. Fill greased muffin tins about three-quarters full. Bake until a wooden skewer inserted in the center comes out clean, about 25 minutes. Turn out onto a wire rack and cool briefly before serving.

Makes 12 muffins.

Orange-Glazed Prune Muffins

1/2 cup vegetable oil
1/2 cup granulated sugar
2 eggs
3/4 cup low-fat buttermilk
3/4 cup unbleached all-purpose flour
1/2 cup whole wheat flour
1 teaspoon baking powder
1/2 teaspoon baking soda

1/4 teaspoon salt
1 teaspoon freshly grated nutmeg
1 teaspoon ground cinnamon
1/2 teaspoon ground allspice
1/2 teaspoon ground cloves
1 cup coarsely mashed cooked pitted prunes (about 20)
1/2 cup chopped pecans or walnuts (optional)

ORANGE GLAZE
3/4 cup powdered sugar
2 tablespoons freshly squeezed orange juice
1 tablespoon grated orange zest

Preheat the oven to 375° F.

Combine the oil, sugar, eggs, and buttermilk in a large bowl, and beat until well blended.

In a separate medium-sized bowl, combine the flours, baking powder, baking soda, salt, nutmeg, cinnamon, allspice, and cloves. Add to the liquid mixture, stirring just enough to blend well. Stir in the prunes and nuts.

Fill greased muffin tins about three-quarters full and bake until the tops are browned and a wooden skewer inserted in the center comes out clean, about 20 minutes.

Meanwhile, to make the glaze, combine the powdered sugar with orange juice and zest; reserve.

Remove the muffins from their tins and turn onto a wire rack to cool for about 5 minutes. While still warm, brush the tops with the reserved Orange Glaze. Serve warm.

Makes 12 muffins.

Spicy Cocoa Muffins

1 3/4 cups unbleached all-purpose flour
3/4 cup granulated sugar
6 tablespoons unsweetened cocoa powder
2 teaspoons baking powder
1/2 teaspoon baking soda
2 teaspoons ground cinnamon
1/4 teaspoon ground cloves
3/4 teaspoon salt
2 eggs, lightly beaten
1 cup low-fat buttermilk
1/2 cup (1 stick) unsalted butter, melted, or
    vegetable oil
1/2 cup finely chopped pecans or walnuts
1/2 cup semisweet chocolate chips (optional)

Preheat the oven to 400° F.

Sift the flour, sugar, cocoa powder, baking powder, baking soda, cinnamon, cloves, and salt together into a large bowl.

In a separate bowl, combine the eggs, buttermilk, and melted butter. Add the liquid mixture to the dry ingredients, stirring just enough to moisten. Fold in the nuts and chocolate chips. Spoon the mixture into greased muffin pans, filling three-quarters full, and bake until a wooden skewer inserted in the center comes out clean, about 15 minutes. Remove immediately from tins and cool briefly on a wire rack.

Makes 12 muffins.

Popovers

For maximum puffiness, avoid overbeating the batter or opening the oven door until the popovers are almost done. Serve piping hot with plenty of butter and jam or honey.

2 eggs
1 cup low-fat milk
1 cup sifted unbleached all-purpose flour
2 teaspoons granulated sugar
1/4 teaspoon salt
2 tablespoons butter, melted

Preheat the oven to 400° F.

Combine the eggs, milk, flour, sugar, and salt, and beat with a wire whisk or in a food processor or blender just enough to blend. Stir in the melted butter. Pour into well-buttered popover pans, muffin tins, or custard cups, filling about half full. Bake until golden brown and firm to the touch, about 35 minutes. If you prefer drier interiors, remove the popovers from the pans or cups and replace them at an angle. Pierce each with a skewer, turn off the heat, and let them stand in the oven, with the door ajar, for about 8 minutes. When done, serve immediately.

Makes 6 large popovers.

Oatmeal Loaf

Try this quick bread with Apple Butter (page 17) or Lemon Curd (page 20).

1 1/2 cups regular (not instant) rolled oats
1 1/2 cups low-fat buttermilk
3/4 cup whole wheat flour
3/4 cup unbleached all-purpose flour
3/4 teaspoon salt
1 1/2 teaspoons ground ginger
3/4 teaspoon freshly ground nutmeg
2 1/2 teaspoons baking powder
1/2 teaspoon baking soda
1/3 cup vegetable oil
1/3 cup maple syrup
2 eggs, lightly beaten
1 cup golden raisins

Combine the oats and buttermilk in a large mixing bowl and let stand to soften the oats, about 30 minutes.

Preheat the oven to 350° F.

In a smaller bowl, combine the flours, salt, ginger, nutmeg, baking powder, and baking soda. Reserve.

Add the oil, syrup, and eggs to the soaked oats and mix well. Add the dry mixture and the raisins, stirring only enough to moisten. Pour into a greased and floured 9 x 5-inch loaf pan and bake until a wooden skewer inserted in the center comes out clean, about 1 hour. Serve warm.

Makes 1 loaf; serves 6 to 8.

Whole Wheat Zucchini Bread

Since this bread keeps for two weeks or longer in the refrigerator and freezes nicely for longer storage, you may wish to multiply the recipe.

2 eggs
1/2 cup vegetable oil
3 tablespoons molasses
1/2 cup packed light brown sugar
1 teaspoon vanilla extract
3/4 cup whole wheat pastry flour
1/2 cup unbleached all-purpose flour
1/2 teaspoon baking soda
1/4 teaspoon baking powder
1/2 teaspoon salt
1 teaspoon ground cinnamon
1 cup shredded zucchini, drained if watery
1/2 cup dried currants or raisins
1/2 cup chopped nuts

Preheat the oven to 350° F.

Beat the eggs in a large mixing bowl. Add the oil, molasses, sugar, and vanilla, and beat until thick and smooth.

In a separate bowl, combine the flours, baking soda, baking powder, salt, and cinnamon. Add to the egg mixture, stirring just until well blended. Fold in the zucchini, currants, and nuts. Pour into a greased and floured 5 x 9-inch loaf pan and bake until a wooden skewer inserted in the center tests clean, about 1 hour. Cool in the pan for 10 minutes before turning onto a wire rack to cool.

Makes 1 loaf; serves 6 to 8.

Buttermilk Biscuits

My aunt, Doris Keith, of Jackson, Mississippi, makes a pan of wonderful hot biscuits almost every morning. Her recipe is very simple; the perfection she exhibits probably comes from the daily practice. While my aunt recommends self-rising flour (which already contains baking powder and salt), I've adapted her recipe to all-purpose flour.

As a youngster, I always asked for "white" biscuits, which meant cooked only until the tops were barely beginning to brown. I still like them this way. If you prefer a browner top, brush the biscuits with melted butter before baking. If you enjoy the sides crusty, arrange the biscuits about 1 inch apart in the baking pan; for soft sides, arrange them touching.

2 cups unbleached all-purpose flour
2 teaspoons baking powder
1/2 teaspoon baking soda
1/2 teaspoon salt
1/2 cup vegetable shortening
3/4 cup low-fat buttermilk

Preheat the oven to 400° F.

Combine the flour, baking powder, baking soda, and salt in a bowl or food processor. Cut in the shortening with a pastry blender or the steel blade (Aunt Doris uses a spoon) until the mixture resembles coarse cornmeal. Add the buttermilk and stir or blend just until the mixture sticks together.

Turn onto a lightly floured surface and knead lightly and quickly, about 30 seconds. Roll out with a lightly floured rolling pin to about 1/4 to 1/2 inch thick. Cut with a 2 1/2-inch floured biscuit cutter. Place in a lightly greased pan. Bake until lightly browned, 10 to 12 minutes. Serve piping hot with butter and good jelly, jam, honey, or syrup.

Makes about 12 biscuits.

Yeast Biscuits

Serve the biscuits piping hot with plenty of butter and good jelly or jam. The dough keeps in the refrigerator for several days. Cut off and roll out only what you need at one time.

1 package (1/4 ounce) quick-rising active dry yeast
5 tablespoons warm water
5 cups unbleached all-purpose flour
5 teaspoons baking powder
1/2 teaspoon baking soda
3 tablespoons granulated sugar
1 teaspoon salt
1 cup vegetable oil
2 cups low-fat buttermilk

Sprinkle the yeast over the warm water in a small bowl, stir, and let stand until soft and foamy, about 5 minutes.

In a bowl or food processor, combine the flour, baking powder, baking soda, sugar, and salt. Cut the oil into the mixture with a pastry blender or the steel blade until the mixture is the texture of coarse cornmeal. Pour in the buttermilk and softened yeast. Stir or blend the mixture quickly to combine the liquid with the dry ingredients. Cover and chill for at least 1 hour, or preferably overnight.

Form the chilled dough into a ball and turn out onto a generously floured surface. Knead lightly and quickly, about 1 minute. Roll out with a lightly floured rolling pin to about 1/2 inch thick. Cut with a 2 1/2-inch round cutter and place barely touching in a lightly greased pan or on a baking sheet. Cover with plastic wrap or a kitchen towel and set aside to rise just until puffy, 20 to 30 minutes.

Preheat the oven to 400° F.

Bake until lightly browned, about 10 to 15 minutes.

Makes about 48 biscuits.

Whole Wheat Scones with Orange Butter

These butter-rich British biscuits are traditionally served with afternoon tea, but they are equally comforting in the morning.

ORANGE BUTTER

2 tablespoons grated orange zest
3 tablespoons powdered sugar
1/2 cup (1 stick) unsalted butter, softened

WHOLE WHEAT SCONES

1 cup whole wheat flour
1 cup unbleached all-purpose flour
3 tablespoons granulated sugar
1 teaspoon baking powder
1/2 teaspoon baking soda
1/2 teaspoon salt
1/2 cup (1 stick) unsalted butter, chilled,
    cut into small pieces
1/3 cup dried currants or raisins
1/3 to 1/2 cup low-fat buttermilk
1/2 teaspoon ground cinnamon, mixed with
    1 teaspoon sugar

To make the Orange Butter, combine the orange zest, powdered sugar, and butter in a food processor or blender and blend until well mixed. Chill until just before serving.

To make the scones, combine the flours, sugar, baking powder, baking soda, and salt in a medium-sized bowl or in a food processor. Cut in the cold butter with a pastry blender or the steel blade until the mixture resembles coarse cornmeal. Stir in the currants by hand, then blend in the buttermilk, 1 tablespoon at a time, just until the mixture is moist enough to hold together.

Preheat the oven to 350° F.

Pat the dough into a ball, flatten on a lightly floured board or pastry cloth, and roll into a circle about 1/4 inch thick. Cut with a floured knife or metal cutter into round, square, or diamond shapes about 2 1/2 inches in diameter. Place on a lightly greased baking sheet and sprinkle with the cinnamon sugar. Bake until golden brown, about 15 to 20 minutes. Serve warm, with the reserved Orange Butter.

Makes about 12 scones.

VARIATION: Use all unbleached white flour for a lighter scone.

Brioches

Here's an easy version of the French classic. In addition to serving them on their own, you can split the brioches and fill them with scrambled eggs, creamed ham or chicken, or other favorite fillings for a main dish.

1 package (1/4 ounce) quick-rising active dry yeast
1/2 cup warm water or milk
5 eggs
3/4 cup (1 1/2 sticks) unsalted butter, softened
1 1/2 tablespoons granulated sugar
1 teaspoon salt
Grated zest of 1 lemon (optional)
2 1/2 cups sifted unbleached all-purpose flour
1 egg yolk
1 tablespoon milk

Sprinkle the yeast over the warm water in a small bowl and let stand until soft and foamy, about 5 minutes.

In a heavy-duty mixer bowl or food processor, combine the eggs, butter, sugar, salt, lemon zest, and the softened yeast, and mix until smooth. Gradually add the flour, mixing until well blended. Gather the dough into a ball, transfer to a lightly oiled bowl, turn the dough to coat all sides with oil, cover the bowl tightly with plastic wrap, and let rise in a warm place until doubled in bulk, about 40 minutes.

Punch the dough down. Pinch off about 3/4 cup of the dough and reserve. Divide the remaining dough into 12 equal pieces and shape each into a smooth round by pulling the surface of the dough to the underside of the round. Place rounds, smooth side up, in well-greased fluted brioche tins or muffin pans, pressing lightly to fit bottoms into the pan.

Divide the reserved dough into 12 pieces and shape with your hands into pear shapes. Poke a hole in the center of each brioche with your finger and firmly insert the small end of the pear-shaped dough pieces into each larger piece of dough. Cover and let stand in a warm place until almost doubled in bulk, about 25 minutes.

Preheat the oven to 375° F.

Combine the egg yolk and milk and gently brush the top of each brioche, being careful to avoid accumulation in the crease where the two pieces of dough are joined. Bake until richly browned, 20 to 25 minutes. Remove from pans and cool briefly on wire racks. Serve warm with unsalted butter and jam.

Makes 12 brioches.

VARIATION: Instead of forming rolls, place the dough in one piece in a 9 x 5 x 3-inch loaf pan, let rise until the dough is about 1 inch from the top of the pan, then bake until richly browned, about 45 minutes. The rich loaf is excellent toasted, turned into ultra-rich French toast, or used for breakfast sandwiches of bacon and eggs or grilled ham and cheese.

Croissants

If you live near a good bakery that makes these flaky French breakfast standbys, you're lucky. If not, here's as simple a process as possible. The technique is easy; it's the chilling between steps that makes the preparation a long one, and the several foldings of the dough that make the rolls flaky. Serve hot with sweet butter and jam.

1 package (1/4 ounce) quick-rising active dry yeast
3/4 cup warm water
1/2 cup milk, warmed
1 cup (2 sticks) unsalted butter, softened
1 tablespoon granulated sugar
1 teaspoon salt
2 3/4 cups sifted unbleached all-purpose flour
1 egg, beaten with 1 tablespoon water

Sprinkle the yeast over the warm water and milk in a large mixing bowl and let stand until soft and foamy, about 5 minutes. Stir in 1 tablespoon of the butter, the sugar, and the salt. Add the flour, mixing just until the mass holds together. Turn out onto a lightly floured surface and knead lightly until the dough is smooth. Roll out into a 1/4-inch-thick rectangle about 9 x 14 inches, with the short side facing you.

Spread the remaining butter over the bottom half of the dough rectangle. Fold the top half over the butter, pressing the edges of the dough together to seal. Place the dough on a lightly floured baking sheet, cover with plastic wrap, and chill for 30 minutes.

Place the chilled dough, with the long sealed side toward the right, on a lightly floured surface and roll out into a rectangle about 1/4 inch thick. Fold the dough over in thirds as you would a letter, wrap with plastic wrap, place on a baking sheet, and refrigerate until well chilled, 30 to 45 minutes.

Place the chilled dough, again with the long sealed side on the right, on a lightly floured surface, and roll out again into a rectangle 1/4 inch thick. Fold in thirds again, wrap, and chill for at least 1 hour or up to several hours.

Repeat the rolling, folding, and chilling two more times. After the final folding, you can refrigerate as long as overnight.

Roll out the dough on a lightly floured surface to a 10 x 20-inch rectangle, lifting the dough and flouring the surface as needed. Trim with a sharp knife to make the edges and corners straight. Using a sharp knife, cut the dough in half lengthwise, then cut each half into 4 equal squares. Cut each square diagonally in half to form 16 triangles.

Starting from the wide end, roll each triangle up and curve the ends to form a crescent shape. With the tip of the triangle tucked underneath, place the croissants about 2 inches apart on buttered baking sheets. Brush the tops and sides with the egg and water mixture, cover, and let rise in a warm place until almost doubled in size, 40 minutes to 1 hour.

Preheat the oven to 425° F.

Gently brush the croissants again with the egg and water glaze. Bake for 10 minutes, then reduce the heat to 375° F. and bake until the croissants are golden brown, about 10 minutes more. Remove and cool briefly on wire racks before serving.

Makes 16 croissants.

NOTE: Wrap and freeze any croissants that will not be eaten on the day they're baked. Place frozen croissants in a preheated 400° F. oven to reheat, about 5 minutes.

Bagels

In some circles, bagels have long been a breakfast favorite when smeared with cream cheese, then topped with lox or smoked salmon. (As an alternative, I enjoy blending cream cheese with chopped smoked salmon and chives for spreading.) Now bagels are rapidly becoming a new American favorite, with bagel shops from coast to coast turning out the chewy rounds with a variety of flavors built in, or spread with almost any filling the imagination can dream up. My favorite way to eat them is split and toasted, with sweet butter and fruit jam.

1 package (1/4 ounce) quick-rising active dry yeast
1 cup warm water
1/4 cup (1/2 stick) unsalted butter, melted, or
**   vegetable oil**
1 1/2 teaspoons salt
2 teaspoons granulated sugar
3 to 3 3/4 cups unbleached all-purpose flour
1 egg, beaten with 1 tablespoon water
Coarse salt or seeds (caraway, sesame, or poppy) for
**   sprinkling (optional)**

Sprinkle the yeast over the warm water in a large bowl and let stand until very soft, about 5 minutes. Add the butter, salt, and sugar, and stir until well blended. Add 2 cups of the flour and beat until the dough is smooth. Slowly add just enough of the remaining flour to make a dough that is firm enough to handle.

Turn the dough out onto a lightly floured surface and knead for about 2 minutes. Let the dough rest for 10 minutes, then continue kneading until the dough is smooth and elastic, about 10 minutes more, sprinkling on additional flour as needed to keep the dough from being sticky. Gather the dough into a ball and place in a greased bowl. Cover and let rise in a warm place until doubled in bulk, about 40 minutes.

Punch the dough down and turn out onto a lightly floured surface. Divide into pieces roughly the size of golf balls, then roll each piece into a smooth ball. Poke your finger through the center of each ball to make a hole. With your finger in the hole, place each circle of dough on a lightly floured surface. Spin your finger around until the hole enlarges and the ring of dough is about 4 inches in diameter. Rest each ring of dough on a floured surface while you complete the remainder.

Preheat the oven to 425° F. and bring 2 to 3 quarts of water to a boil in a large pot or Dutch oven.

Drop the dough rings, 3 or 4 at a time, into the boiling water. Cook until they float to the surface, about 3 minutes, then turn and cook on the other side for about 3 minutes more. Remove with a slotted spoon and transfer to greased baking sheets, placing the bagels about 1 inch apart. When all the bagels have been boiled, brush the tops with the egg and water mixture. Sprinkle with coarse salt or selected seeds if desired. Bake until lightly golden, about 15 minutes. Remove to wire racks to cool.

Makes 15 to 18 bagels.

VARIATIONS: For whole wheat bagels, substitute whole wheat flour for about one-third of the all-purpose flour; bake a few minutes longer.

To make egg bagels, add 3 beaten egg yolks along with the butter.

Butter-Rich Waffles

On those occasions when indulging is justified, try these delectable waffles that were a special favorite of my good friend, Martha Jane Cotton. Although I like to cook waffles in a deep-pocketed Belgian waffle iron, any type of waffle iron will do. For a romantic change of pace, try the heart-shaped Scandinavian waffle maker. No matter what iron, be sure to season the grids according to the manufacturer's directions before adding the batter.

2 eggs, separated
1 1/2 cups milk
2 teaspoons baking powder
1 cup sifted unbleached all-purpose flour
1/2 cup (1 stick) unsalted butter, melted

Preheat a waffle iron.

In a bowl, beat the egg whites until stiff but not dry. Reserve.

In a separate bowl, food processor, or blender, combine the egg yolks, milk, baking powder, flour, and melted butter and beat until smooth. Fold in the reserved egg whites. Bake according to directions on your waffle iron. Serve hot with your favorite toppings.

Serves 4.

VARIATIONS: Inspired by a waffle created by Bradley Ogden that I enjoyed at the Campton Place restaurant in San Francisco: add 1/2 to 3/4 cup chopped toasted macadamia nuts to the batter. Serve with melted butter mixed with freshly grated coconut and top the waffles with additional toasted macadamias.

When you're being health or diet conscious, substitute whole wheat pastry flour for the all-purpose variety. Use honey instead of sugar if you prefer, and cut back on the butter, or use about 1/2 cup vegetable oil instead.

Add 1/2 to 3/4 cup chopped pecans or other nuts, toasted sunflower seeds, or crumbled bacon to the batter.

Substitute buttermilk, sour cream, or yogurt for the milk, and add 1 teaspoon baking soda along with the baking powder.

Four-Grain Pancakes

The ingredients list would lead you to think these will be heavy, but they turn out light and scrumptious. Add seasonal berries or chopped bananas to the batter if you wish.

1 1/2 cups regular (not instant) rolled oats
3/4 cup buckwheat flour
3/4 cup whole wheat flour
3/4 cup polenta or coarse yellow cornmeal
4 teaspoons baking powder
1 1/2 teaspoons baking soda
4 1/2 cups low-fat buttermilk
1/4 cup maple syrup
2 eggs, lightly beaten, or 4 egg whites, lightly beaten
1/3 cup vegetable oil

Combine the oats, buckwheat flour, whole wheat flour, polenta, baking powder, and baking soda in a large mixing bowl.

In a separate large bowl, combine the buttermilk, syrup, eggs, and oil, and beat until well blended. Add the dry ingredients and blend together quickly. Allow to stand to soften the grains before baking, about 15 minutes.

Preheat a griddle or large heavy skillet.

Lightly oil the griddle and spoon or pour the batter, about 1/3 cup for each pancake, onto it and cook until the tops are bubbly; turn and cook until lightly browned on the other side. Serve piping hot with your favorite toppings.

Serves 6 to 8.

Lemon Soufflé Pancakes

Good for weight watchers, these light-as-air pancakes also taste great.

6 eggs, separated
2 cups small-curd cottage cheese
1/4 cup vegetable oil
2 tablespoons maple syrup or granulated sugar
1/2 teaspoon salt
4 teaspoons freshly squeezed lemon juice, preferably
     from Meyer variety
4 teaspoons baking powder
1 cup unbleached all-purpose flour

Preheat a griddle or a large heavy skillet.

In a bowl, beat the egg whites until stiff but not dry. Reserve.

Combine the cottage cheese, egg yolks, oil, syrup, salt, lemon juice, baking powder, and flour in a food processor or blender and blend until smooth. Fold in the egg whites. Lightly oil the griddle, spoon on the batter, about 3 tablespoons for each pancake, and bake until the tops are bubbly. Turn and cook until bottoms are done. Serve hot with your favorite toppings.

Serves 4 to 6.

VARIATION: Add about 1 cup chopped banana, chopped papaya, grated apple, berries, or other fruit to the batter.

Round Danish Pancakes (Aebleskiver)

Aebleskiver must be cooked in special pans that can be purchased at hardware or kitchenware stores. Serve with fruit jam, warm applesauce, warm honey, or maple syrup.

2 eggs, separated
2 cups low-fat buttermilk
2 cups unbleached all-purpose flour
2 tablespoons granulated sugar
2 teaspoons baking powder
1/2 teaspoon baking soda
1/2 teaspoon salt
1/2 teaspoon ground cardamom or vanilla extract
1/4 cup (1/2 stick) unsalted butter, melted
Vegetable oil
Powdered sugar

Beat the egg whites in a medium-sized bowl until stiff but not dry. Reserve.

Combine the egg yolks, buttermilk, flour, sugar, baking powder, baking soda, salt, cardamom, and melted butter in a bowl, and mix until smooth. Fold in the beaten egg whites.

Preheat the oven to 200° F.

Pour about 3/4 teaspoon oil into each round of an *aebleskiver* pan and heat over medium-high heat. Add a heaping tablespoon of the batter, or enough to fill each round about three-quarters full. When bubbly around the edges, turn each round upside down with chopsticks or a fork. Continue cooking, turning frequently, until the rounds are golden on all sides and done in the middle, about 5 minutes. Remove each cake as it is done and drain on paper towels. Keep warm in the oven until all rounds are cooked. Sprinkle with powdered sugar and serve warm with selected topping.

Serves 6 to 8.

Johnnycakes

This New England tradition is best made with hard white flint corn, although any stone-ground cornmeal may be used. Both types of cornmeal are available in natural-foods stores and some supermarkets. Use plenty of butter on the griddle in order for the cakes to form crunchy crusts in contrast with the soft interiors. Serve hot with melted butter and warm maple syrup.

1 cup white flint corn or other stone-ground cornmeal
1/2 teaspoon salt
3/4 cup boiling water
2 tablespoons unsalted butter, melted
2 teaspoons granulated sugar
1/4 cup milk or light cream (or half-and-half)
Butter or vegetable oil for cooking

Preheat a griddle or large heavy skillet to medium.

Combine the cornmeal and salt in a bowl, then gradually add the boiling water, stirring constantly with a wire whisk or wooden spoon to prevent lumps. Stir in the melted butter, sugar, and milk.

Brush the preheated griddle generously with butter or oil. Drop the batter by heaping tablespoons onto the griddle and cook until crisp and golden on each side, 5 to 8 minutes per side. Add more butter or oil as needed.

Serves 4.

Blueberry Corn Pancakes

These are my very favorite pancakes. The golden color and crunchy texture of the corn are counterpointed by dark and juicy blueberries. When fresh berries are not available, unsweetened frozen ones work well. Serve hot with melted butter and warm maple syrup.

1 1/2 cups polenta or coarse yellow cornmeal
1/4 cup whole wheat flour
1 teaspoon baking soda
1/2 teaspoon salt
2 tablespoons maple syrup or honey
2 tablespoons vegetable oil
2 cups low-fat buttermilk
1 egg, lightly beaten
About 1 1/2 cups fresh blueberries, stemmed and
**   picked over**

Combine the cornmeal, flour, baking soda, and salt in a medium-sized bowl.

In a small bowl, combine the syrup, oil, buttermilk, and egg. Stir well, and quickly mix into the dry ingredients. Let stand for 10 minutes to soften the cornmeal.

Preheat a griddle or a large heavy skillet.

Lightly grease the hot griddle, and pour on the batter, about 1/4 cup for each pancake. Then sprinkle the tops with the blueberries, and cook until the tops are bubbly. Turn and cook until golden on the other side.

Serves 4.

Low-Calorie Toppings for Breakfast Treats

Waffles, pancakes, and French toast need not call for loads of fattening syrups, although just a drizzle of maple or other favorite syrup is okay and quite satisfactory. Here are alternatives:

Puréed seasonal fruit, plain or with cinnamon or other spices; great heated briefly in a microwave oven.

Apples, bananas, pears, or other fruits sautéed in a little butter.

Unsweetened applesauce; especially good warmed.

Cottage cheese puréed with fresh or cooked fruit.

A squeeze of lemon juice and a light sprinkling of powdered sugar.

Unsweetened fruit conserves (available in natural-foods stores and some supermarkets).

Puffed Oven-Baked Pancakes

Known by such picturesque names as "Dutch Babies" and "Bismarks," these showy German classics are among my favorite breakfast treats for entertaining. The basic recipe is for individual pancakes as shown on the cover. For larger groups, multiply all ingredients as you increase the pan size. I've baked awe-inspiring giant versions in a shallow paella pan that holds eight times the batter recipe.

The classic topping is a sprinkling of powdered sugar and a generous squeeze from lemon wedges. Other suggestions follow the recipe. No matter which toppings you choose, present them in small bowls at the table for adding according to taste. Be sure to have the whole breakfast on the table and everyone seated before bringing the pancake directly from the oven.

2 tablespoons unsalted butter
1 egg
1/4 cup low-fat milk
1/4 cup unbleached all-purpose flour
1/4 teaspoon almond extract (optional)
1/2 teaspoon grated lemon zest (optional)
Toppings

Preheat the oven to 475° F.

Place the butter in a 4-inch ovenproof skillet, ramekin, or other baking dish, and heat in the oven until the butter is melted.

While the butter melts, beat the egg in a food processor, blender, or bowl with a wire whisk until light and bright yellow. Gradually beat in the milk, then the flour, until smooth. Stir in the almond extract and lemon zest. Pour the batter into the pan of hot butter and return the pan to the oven. Cook until the pancake is puffed and golden, about 12 minutes. Serve at once, accompanied by selected toppings. When you make larger pancakes, cut them into wedges at the table, or spread with selected topping, roll up jelly-roll fashion, and cut crosswise into slices at the table.

Serves 1.

TOPPINGS

Powdered sugar and fresh lemon juice.

Sliced fresh berries or other seasonal fruit.

Warmed applesauce or chestnut purée.

Berry Butter (page 22).

Apple, banana, papaya, or pear slices sautéed in butter.

Dried fruits reconstituted in boiling water.

Butter-toasted sliced almonds.

Oven-toasted chopped pecans or walnuts.

Butter-toasted chopped macadamia nuts with freshly grated coconut.

Skillet Cake with Sautéed Apples

Cooking teacher Babs Retzer introduced this recipe into my repertoire of foods for entertaining.

7 tablespoons unsalted butter
4 or 5 Red or Golden Delicious apples, cored and thinly sliced
3/4 cup packed brown sugar
3 eggs, separated
1/2 teaspoon baking soda
1 cup low-fat buttermilk
1 cup unbleached all-purpose flour
1 teaspoon baking powder
1/4 teaspoon salt
1/2 pint (1 cup) sour cream

Melt 6 tablespoons of the butter in a sauté pan or skillet over medium heat. Add the apples and sauté until they are tender but still hold their shape, about 10 minutes, covering for the last few minutes. When almost done, stir in the brown sugar. Reserve and keep warm.

Beat the egg whites in a bowl until stiff but not dry. Reserve.

In a medium-sized bowl, dissolve the baking soda in the buttermilk. Beat the egg yolks and add them to the buttermilk. Stir in the flour, baking powder, and salt. Then fold in the egg whites.

Preheat the broiler.

Melt the remaining 1 tablespoon of butter in a 10-inch skillet over medium heat. Add the batter and cook until set, 3 to 5 minutes. Place the skillet about 4 inches under the preheated broiler and continue cooking until the top is lightly browned. Test with a wooden skewer; if not dry, place over low heat and cook until done.

Turn the cake onto a very large serving platter. Surround the cake with the sautéed apples and top them with sour cream. Cut into wedges to serve.

Serves 4.

Monkey Bread

This is a special delight to children of all ages. Use your favorite recipe for whole wheat bread, or purchase a good brand of frozen honey-wheat bread dough. For the ultimate sensation, use the dough for Croissants (page 34). If using frozen dough, thaw it overnight in the refrigerator; it will be ready to use in the morning.

3/4 cup granulated sugar
3/4 cup packed light brown sugar
2 teaspoons ground cinnamon
Dough for 3 loaves honey-sweetened whole wheat
        bread, risen, or 3 loaves good-quality frozen
        commercial honey-wheat bread dough, thawed
About 1/2 cup (1 stick) unsalted butter, melted

Heavily grease a 10-inch tube cake pan.

Combine the sugar, brown sugar, and cinnamon in a shallow bowl. Mix well.

With flour-dusted hands, tear off pieces of risen dough about 1 1/2 inches in diameter. Roll each piece into a round ball. Dip a dough ball into the melted butter, then roll in the cinnamon sugar until completely coated, and place in the pan. Continue to coat the balls and place in the pan about 1/2 inch apart, layering until the dough is used or the pan is about three-quarters full. Cover with a cloth kitchen towel and let stand in a warm place until the dough rises to the top of the pan, about 30 minutes.

Preheat the oven to 350° F.

Bake until a wooden skewer tests clean when inserted in the center, about 1 hour, covering loosely with foil if the top begins to get too brown. Remove from the oven and let cool for 5 to 10 minutes, then unmold and serve warm. To eat, pull the loaf apart.

44

Serves 6 to 10.

VARIATION: Raisins and/or chopped nuts may be sprinkled between layers and on top of the dough.

Toast Toppings

Turn routine morning toast into something special by topping it with one of the following combinations before grilling in a toaster oven until the topping is bubbly. Or lightly brown one side of the bread under a broiler, then turn and add topping to the other side and heat until the topping is bubbly.

Spread top side with unsalted butter and generously sprinkle with ground cinnamon and granulated sugar to taste.

Spread top side with unsalted butter or peanut butter, then cover with sliced bananas and drizzle with honey.

Spread top side lightly with butter, then cover with sliced or shredded cheese. Sprinkle with cayenne pepper to taste.

Spread top side with unsalted butter, then cover with finely chopped nuts and drizzle with honey.

Spread top side with Berry Butter (page 20).

Sticky Buns

Gooey glazed cinnamon rolls are the current rage at bakeries coast to coast. They're easy to make at home, and the whole wheat and wheat germ give them more nutrition than their bakery counterparts.

SWEET YEAST DOUGH

2 packages (1/4 ounce *each*) quick-rising active
    dry yeast
1/4 cup warm water
3 eggs, at room temperature
1/3 cup granulated sugar
2 teaspoons salt
1/2 teaspoon baking soda
1 cup low-fat buttermilk
1/2 cup (1 stick) unsalted butter, melted, or
    vegetable oil
3 3/4 cups unbleached all-purpose flour
2 cups whole wheat pastry flour
1/4 cup wheat germ

CURRANT-PECAN FILLING

1 1/2 cups packed brown sugar
1/2 cup (1 stick) unsalted butter, softened
1 1/2 tablespoons ground cinnamon
1/2 cup dried currants
3/4 cup finely chopped pecans

STICKY PECAN GLAZE

1 cup (2 sticks) unsalted butter, softened
1 3/4 cups packed brown sugar
1/4 cup dark corn syrup
3/4 cup small pecan halves or coarsely chopped pecans

To make the dough, sprinkle the yeast over the warm water in a small bowl, stir, and let stand until soft, about 5 minutes. Reserve.

In a large bowl, combine the eggs, sugar, salt, baking soda, buttermilk, and butter, and beat until smooth. Stir in the reserved yeast.

In a separate bowl, combine the flours and wheat germ. Then add 3 cups of the dry mixture to the wet ingredients, beating until well blended. Add 2 more cups of the dry ingredients and beat until the dough just holds together. Turn out onto a lightly floured surface and knead for 1 minute. Let the dough rest for 10 minutes.

Knead the dough again, sprinkling on the remainder of the flour mixture as needed, until smooth and elastic, about 10 minutes. Place in a greased bowl, turn, cover with plastic wrap, and let rise in a warm place until about doubled in bulk, about 40 minutes.

Meanwhile, to make the filling, combine the brown sugar, butter, cinnamon, currants, and pecans in a bowl, and mix thoroughly. Reserve.

To make the glaze, combine the butter, brown sugar, and corn syrup in a bowl, and beat until well mixed. Spread the mixture evenly over the bottom of a buttered 10 x 15-inch baking pan. Sprinkle evenly with the pecans and set aside.

Punch the risen dough down and turn it out onto a lightly floured surface. Roll out into a 15 x 24-inch rectangle about 1/2 inch thick. Sprinkle the reserved filling over the dough, gently pressing the mixture into the dough with your fingers. Beginning with the short end, roll the dough up like a jelly roll. Slice crosswise into 12 equal pieces. Place the slices, cut side down and barely touching each other, on top of the glaze in the pan. Cover, and let rise in a warm place until puffy and almost doubled in bulk, about 25 minutes.

Preheat the oven to 375° F.   *(continued)*

Bake the buns until golden brown on top, 25 to 30 minutes. Remove from the oven and cool in the pan to set the glaze, about 5 minutes. Invert onto a serving tray or another baking sheet and allow glaze to dribble down the sides. Pull apart and serve warm.

Makes 12 large buns.

VARIATIONS: For a lighter bun, substitute more all-purpose flour for the whole wheat and the wheat germ. For cinnamon buns, omit the Sticky Pecan Glaze, bake in a buttered pan, then brush with a mixture of 3/4 cup powdered sugar, 1 tablespoon warm water, and 1 tablespoon freshly squeezed lemon juice.

Filled Raised Coffeecake

This big, moist coffeecake is based on my recollections of the Russian coffeecake I used to buy each weekend at Zabar's in New York. This is a good recipe for entertaining a crowd.

Sweet Yeast Dough (page 46)
1 teaspoon powdered saffron (optional)
3 cups golden raisins, plumped in hot water, brandy,
    or rum and drained
2 cups canned juice-packed crushed pineapple,
    drained
3 tablespoons grated orange zest
2 tablespoons grated lemon zest
2 1/2 cups chopped pecans
1 cup packed light brown sugar
2 tablespoons ground cinnamon
1 1/2 cups (3 sticks) unsalted butter, softened

Make the yeast dough for Sticky Buns as on page 46, adding the saffron along with the yeast if desired. Then follow all steps through the first rising.

Meanwhile, to make the filling, drain the raisins and combine them with the drained pineapple and orange and lemon zests in a bowl; reserve.

In a small bowl, combine the nuts, brown sugar, and cinnamon; reserve.

Punch the risen dough down and turn out onto a lightly floured surface. Divide the dough into 2 equal pieces, then roll out each piece to fit into a 9 x 13-inch baking pan. Grease the pan and place one sheet of dough in the bottom. Spread with half of the softened butter, then sprinkle with half of the raisin mixture and half of the nut mixture. Cover with the second sheet of rolled dough, then spread with the remaining butter and top with the remaining raisin mixture and nut mixture. Cover with a clean cloth towel and let rise in a warm place until the dough is puffy, about 25 minutes.

Preheat the oven to 375° F.

Bake the risen coffee cake until the dough is golden brown and a skewer tests clean when inserted in the center, 30 to 40 minutes. (Cover loosely with foil if the top is getting too brown.) Remove from the oven and cool slightly before serving. To serve, cut into squares.

Serves 12 to 15.

Sour Cream Breakfast Cake with Pecan and Cinnamon Filling

The aroma from the oven as this easy cake bakes will arouse even the laziest person in the house.

PECAN AND CINNAMON FILLING
1 1/2 cup chopped pecans
3/4 cup packed brown sugar
1 tablespoon ground cinnamon

SOUR CREAM CAKE
2 cups unbleached all-purpose flour
1 cup whole wheat pastry flour
1 tablespoon baking powder
1 teaspoon baking soda
1/2 teaspoon salt
1 cup (2 sticks) unsalted butter, softened
1 1/2 cups granulated sugar
1 1/2 cups sour cream
3 eggs
1 1/2 teaspoons grated lemon zest
Powdered sugar for dusting

To prepare the filling, combine the pecans, brown sugar, and cinnamon in a bowl and stir to mix well. Reserve.

Preheat the oven to 350° F.

To prepare the cake, sift together the flours, baking powder, baking soda, and salt in a large bowl.

In a separate bowl, cream the butter, sugar, and sour cream until light and fluffy. Add the eggs, one at a time, beating well after each addition. Stir in the lemon zest. Add the reserved dry ingredients and beat just until smooth.

Pour about half of the batter into a greased and floured 10-inch bundt or tube pan. Sprinkle the reserved filling evenly down the center of the batter, preventing the filling from touching the sides of the pan. Cover with the remaining batter. Bake until a wooden skewer tests clean when inserted in the thickest part, 45 to 55 minutes.

Cool in the pan for 10 minutes before turning out. Dust with powdered sugar before serving.

Makes 1 10-inch bundt cake; serves 8 to 12.

Upside-Down Breakfast Cake

The elegant look of this cake belies the quick and easy technique. If you use blueberries or blackberries, add lemon juice and zest in the batter; when you choose cranberries, use the orange juice and zest. Serve with cream for pouring over the cake, or unsweetened whipped cream, plain yogurt, or a custard sauce.

1/2 cup (1 stick) plus 2 tablespoons unsalted butter,
    softened
1 cup packed light brown sugar
2 1/2 cups fresh blueberries, blackberries, or
    cranberries
1 1/2 cups unbleached all-purpose flour
2 1/2 teaspoons baking powder
1/2 teaspoon salt
3/4 cup granulated sugar
2 eggs
1/4 cup freshly squeezed lemon juice, or
    1/2 cup freshly squeezed orange juice
1/3 cup low-fat milk
1/2 teaspoon vanilla extract
1 tablespoon grated lemon zest, or
    2 tablespoons grated orange zest

Preheat the oven to 350° F.

Combine 2 tablespoons of the butter and the brown sugar in a small bowl, then spread the mixture evenly in the bottom of a lightly greased 9-inch round cake pan. Spread the berries over the mixture and set aside.

Combine the flour, baking powder, and salt in a bowl. Reserve.

In a separate bowl, combine the remaining 1/2 cup butter, the sugar, and the eggs, and beat until creamy smooth. Add the reserved dry ingredients, lemon or orange juice, milk, vanilla, and lemon or orange zest, and beat until well blended. Pour the batter over the berries and bake until the top is golden and a skewer tests clean when inserted in the center, 50 to 55 minutes. Remove from the oven, run a knife around the inside edge of the pan, cover the cake with a serving plate, and invert the cake onto the plate, fruit side up. Cool slightly before serving warm.

Makes 1 9-inch cake; serves 8 to 12.

Creamy Rice Pudding

This cross between rice pudding and *crème brûlée* makes a memorable ending to a holiday or weekend breakfast.

3/4 cup long-grain brown or white rice,
    preferably basmati
1 1/2 cups water
6 egg yolks
1/4 cup granulated sugar
2 1/4 cups heavy (whipping) cream, heated
Brown sugar

Place the rice and water in a saucepan over high heat and bring to a boil. Cover, reduce the heat to very low, and simmer until the rice is tender and the water is absorbed, 45 minutes for brown rice or 15 minutes for white rice. Remove from the heat and cool.

Preheat the oven to 250° F.

In a medium-sized bowl, beat the egg yolks and sugar with a wire whisk, then gradually add the hot cream and beat until smooth. Add the rice, stirring to blend thoroughly. Pour the mixture into an ovenproof glass 9-inch pie plate or other shallow dish set in a larger pan. Add boiling water to halfway up the side of the pie pan. Bake until the custard is set and a knife inserted in the center comes out clean, about 1 hour. Remove from the oven and cool, then refrigerate until thoroughly chilled, as long as overnight.

One or 2 hours before serving, preheat the broiler.

Sprinkle the top of the custard with a thin even layer of brown sugar. Using a mister, spray the sugar with a little water. Heat under the preheated broiler until the sugar melts and the tops are bubbly, about 1 minute. Chill at least 20 minutes or up to 2 hours before serving. Cut into wedges.

Serves 8.

Indian Pudding

America's oldest pudding adds a new dimension to the breakfast menu.

1/2 cup yellow cornmeal
1/2 cup molasses
4 cups low-fat milk, heated almost to boiling
2 tablespoons unsalted butter, melted
1 teaspoon ground cinnamon
1 teaspoon ground ginger
1/2 teaspoon ground allspice
1/2 teaspoon salt
2 eggs, lightly beaten
Heavy (whipping) cream

Preheat the oven to 350° F.

Combine the cornmeal and the molasses in the top part of a double boiler, then stir in the hot milk until well blended and smooth. Place over 2 inches of simmering water in the bottom of the double boiler and cook, stirring constantly, until thick and smooth, about 15 minutes. Remove the top portion of the boiler from the heat and stir in the melted butter, the spices, and the salt. Add the eggs and beat until well blended.

Pour the mixture into a generously buttered 1 1/2-quart baking dish, place in a larger pan, and pour about 1 inch boiling water into the larger pan. Bake, stirring occasionally, until set, about 2 hours. Serve warm, with cream to pour over the top.

Serves 6.

Breakfast Bread Pudding with Warm Berry Sauce

It may sound decadent for breakfast, but a warm bread pudding can be a comforting way to begin a special wintry day. The ingredients provide the same nutrition —eggs, dairy products, carbohydrates, fruit—as French toast or many other breakfast favorites. Although richer-tasting with the butter added, a successful light version can be made by using only low-fat milk and omitting the butter, as I accidentally discovered on a morning when there was no cream and I found the melted butter still in the microwave after baking the pudding for a guest. We felt justified in eating hearty portions.

BREAD PUDDING

2 eggs
3/4 cup granulated sugar
3 cups low-fat milk
1 cup heavy (whipping) cream or light cream
    (or half-and-half)
1/2 cup (1 stick) unsalted butter, melted
1 tablespoon vanilla extract
3/4 cup dried currants or raisins
1 teaspoon freshly grated nutmeg
8 ounces stale French bread, preferably whole wheat,
    sliced 1/2 inch thick

WARM BERRY SAUCE

2 cups fresh or frozen raspberries
2 cups fresh or frozen strawberries
1/3 cup granulated sugar
1/3 cup freshly squeezed orange juice
3 tablespoons freshly squeezed lemon juice

Powdered sugar for dusting
Whole fresh raspberries and strawberries for garnish

To make the pudding, combine the eggs, sugar, milk, cream, melted butter, vanilla, currants, and nutmeg in a bowl; whisk to blend well. Pour the mixture over the bread slices in a large bowl and let stand, turning bread as necessary, until bread is soft and saturated, about 20 minutes.

Preheat the oven to 350° F.

Arrange the bread slices in a lightly greased 4-quart baking dish and pour any unabsorbed custard mixture over the bread. Bake, uncovered, until the custard is set and top is lightly browned, about 45 minutes.

To make the sauce, combine the berries, sugar, and orange and lemon juices in a saucepan over medium heat. Cook, stirring continuously, until the fruit begins to break up, about 5 minutes. Purée in a food processor or blender, return to the saucepan, and heat until warm.

To serve, dust the top of the pudding with powdered sugar. Pass the warm sauce and fresh berries at the table.

Serves 8.

French Toast

The French call it *pain perdu,* or "lost bread," because it's made with leftover bread that would otherwise be discarded—or perhaps because it's hidden in batter. In addition to classic French bread, try making this with whole wheat cinnamon bread, hearty grain breads, or stale croissants. Top with honey, syrup, preserves, or other favorite toppings.

4 eggs
1 cup milk
1 tablespoon granulated sugar, honey, or maple syrup
1/4 teaspoon salt
1 teaspoon ground cinnamon
1 teaspoon freshly grated nutmeg
1 tablespoon minced fresh tarragon, or 1 teaspoon
    dried tarragon, crumbled (optional)
1/2 teaspoon vanilla extract
8 slices (1 1/2 inches thick) day-old French-style bread,
    sweet or sourdough
About 1/2 cup (1 stick) unsalted butter
Powdered sugar for dusting

In a large bowl, combine the eggs, milk, sugar or other sweetener, salt, cinnamon, nutmeg, tarragon, and vanilla extract, and beat until well mixed. Dip the bread slices into the mixture, turning to thoroughly coat both sides.

Heat 2 tablespoons of the butter in a skillet over medium heat until foamy. Add half of the bread slices and cook until golden brown on each side, turning once and adding additional butter as needed. Cook the remaining bread in the same way. Dust with powdered sugar and serve hot with your favorite topping.

Serves 4.

Fried Polenta

Use leftovers of this Italian treat from dinner, or make it ahead just to have on hand for breakfast. Use the same technique with grits (ground hominy corn). Serve warm with warmed honey or maple syrup.

6 cups water
1 tablespoon salt
2 cups polenta or coarsely ground yellow cornmeal
1/2 cup (1 stick) unsalted butter

In a copper polenta pan or deep saucepan, bring the water to a boil over high heat. Add the salt and reduce the heat so the water is at a simmer. While stirring continuously with a long-handled wooden spoon, add the polenta in a slow, steady stream. Cook, stirring quite frequently, until polenta is thick enough for the spoon to stand upright, about 15 to 20 minutes. Cut 4 tablespoons (1/2 stick) of the butter into small pieces, add to the polenta, and stir until the butter melts. Pour the polenta into a lightly greased 9 x 5-inch loaf pan, pressing it evenly into the corners. Cover with plastic wrap and refrigerate overnight or up to 3 days.

To remove the polenta loaf, briefly dip the pan into hot water and slide a blunt knife around the edges. Invert the polenta onto a flat surface and remove the pan. Slice the loaf as you would bread.

Preheat the oven to 200° F.

In a large skillet over medium-high heat, melt the remaining butter, about 2 tablespoons at a time as needed, until foamy. Add a few polenta slices at a time and fry until golden brown on one side, about 8 to 10 minutes. Turn and brown the other side, about 8 to 10 minutes more. Transfer to an ovenproof dish and keep warm in the oven until all the slices are cooked, adding the remaining butter as needed.

Serves 6.

New Orleans Raised Rice Cakes
(Calas)

In old New Orleans, black women roamed the French Quarter streets calling *"Belle cala! Tout chaud!"* ("Lovely rice! Piping hot!") The word *cala* is derived from an African word for rice. Cook the rice the night before and combine it with yeast to rise overnight.

1/2 cup long-grain white rice
1 1/2 cups cold water
1 teaspoon salt
1 package (1/4 ounce) active dry yeast
1/2 cup warm water
1/4 cup granulated sugar
1 teaspoon ground cinnamon
1 teaspoon freshly grated nutmeg
1 1/4 cups unbleached all-purpose flour
3 eggs, well beaten
Vegetable oil for deep frying
Powdered sugar for dusting
Dark cane syrup or strawberry jam

Combine the rice, cold water, and salt in a heavy saucepan and bring to a boil over high heat. Cover the pan, reduce the heat to low, and simmer until the rice is very soft, about 25 minutes. Drain off any excess water and transfer the rice to a large bowl. Mash the rice with a wooden spoon and cool to room temperature.

Dissolve the yeast in the warm water, then add it to the rice, stirring to thoroughly combine. Cover the bowl with plastic wrap or a clean cloth towel and set in a warm place to rise overnight.

In the morning, add the sugar, cinnamon, nutmeg, flour, and eggs to the rice. Beat well, cover the bowl, and set in a warm place to rise for about 30 minutes.

Pour oil in a deep fryer or saucepan to a depth of about 3 inches. Heat to 375° F. Preheat the oven to 200° F.

With moistened hands, take about 1 tablespoon of the dough and roll it into a ball. Drop a few at a time into the hot oil and fry, turning frequently with a slotted spoon, until they are golden brown and crusty. Remove with a slotted spoon and drain on paper towels in the warm oven while you fry the remainder. Dust with powdered sugar and serve hot with a pitcher of Louisiana cane syrup or strawberry jam.

Serves 6.

French Doughnut Squares
(Beignets)

During my years in New Orleans, my favorite breakfast—no matter what time of day or night—was a steaming mug of *café au lait* and a plate of powdered-sugar-dusted *beignets* in the French Market. This is as close as I can come to the old Morning Call and Café du Monde originals.

If you can't use all the dough at one time, store it unrolled in the refrigerator for up to five days, breaking off and rolling only what you need at a time.

3/4 cup warm water
1/2 package (1/8 ounce) quick-rising active dry yeast
1/4 cup granulated sugar
1/2 teaspoon salt
1/2 cup canned evaporated milk
1 egg, lightly beaten
2 tablespoons vegetable shortening
3 1/2 cups unbleached all-purpose flour
Vegetable oil for deep frying
Powdered sugar for dusting

Place the water in a shallow bowl, sprinkle with the yeast, stir to dissolve, and let stand until soft and foamy, about 5 minutes.

In a large bowl, combine the sugar, salt, evaporated milk, egg, and shortening. Stir in the yeast and mix thoroughly. Gradually add the flour, about 1 1/2 cups at a time, mixing until well blended; use your fingers if the dough becomes too stiff to stir. Cover the bowl with plastic wrap and refrigerate for several hours or as long as overnight.

Pour vegetable oil into a deep fryer or heavy pot to a depth of 3 inches and heat to 360° F.

Gather the chilled dough into a ball and pat or roll it out on a lightly floured surface to a thickness of about 1/4 inch. Using a sharp knife, cut the dough into 2 x 3-inch rectangles. Drop three at a time into the hot oil, turning them several times with tongs or a slotted spoon until they are golden brown on all sides. Remove with a slotted spoon and drain on paper towels. Sprinkle generously with powdered sugar and serve immediately, with mugs of *café au lait* or strong coffee.

Makes about 36 *beignets*.

DAIRY & EGGS

Breakfast Custard

If you enjoy the flavor of maple as much as I do, use maple sugar and syrup for a change of pace in this classic French custard inspired by a Julia Child recipe. Serve warm or cold, plain or with seasonal fruit.

CARAMEL GLAZE

1/2 cup granulated sugar or granulated maple sugar
2 tablespoons water

CUSTARD

2 1/2 cups low-fat milk
1 vanilla bean, split, or 1 teaspoon vanilla extract
1/2 cup granulated sugar or maple syrup
3 eggs
3 egg yolks
Fresh berries and sliced fruits (optional)

To make the Caramel Glaze, combine the sugar and water in a saucepan over medium-high heat and stir with a wooden spoon until the sugar dissolves. Continue to cook, stirring occasionally or shaking the pan in a circular motion, until the syrup is light brown and caramelized, about 3 minutes. Immediately remove from the heat and pour into a warmed ovenproof 1-quart porcelain or glass dish, turning the dish in all directions to coat the bottom and sides with the caramel until the caramel is hard. Set aside.

To make the custard, heat the milk and the vanilla bean in a saucepan over medium heat and bring just to a simmer. (If you are using vanilla extract, do not add it yet.) Remove from the heat, cover, and set aside.

Preheat the oven to 325° F.

Combine the sugar or maple syrup, eggs, and egg yolks in a mixing bowl, and beat until well blended and foamy. While beating, slowly drizzle in the hot milk; discard the vanilla bean. (Stir in the vanilla extract if you did not use the bean.) Strain the mixture through a wire sieve into the caramel-coated dish and place the dish in a large pan on the lower rack of the oven. Pour enough hot, *not boiling,* water into the large pan to come halfway up the sides of the dish. Bake until a knife tests clean when inserted in the center, 40 to 50 minutes. Watch the water in the pan and adjust the oven temperature to prevent the water from simmering, which will turn the custard grainy.

To serve warm, place the dish in a container of cold water until the custard is firm, about 10 minutes. Run a knife around the edge of the custard, cover the top with a serving plate, and quickly invert the custard. Surround with fresh fruit, or serve the fruit alongside, if desired.

To serve cold, cover and refrigerate the custard until chilled, then unmold as above.

Serves 4 to 6.

Cheese Blintzes

These Jewish crêpes can be filled and refrigerated up to 24 hours ahead. Brown them in butter just before serving with sour cream and your favorite preserves.

CHEESE FILLING
1 small package (3 ounces) cream cheese, softened
1 cup (about 1/2 pound) fresh farmer's (or pot) cheese or small-curd cottage cheese
3 tablespoons granulated sugar
1 egg yolk, well beaten
3/4 teaspoon vanilla extract
1 teaspoon grated lemon zest

CRÊPES
1 cup sifted unbleached all-purpose flour
1/4 teaspoon salt
1 cup water or low-fat milk
2 eggs, well beaten
About 1/2 cup (1 stick) unsalted butter for greasing pan

Sour cream or crème fraîche
Fruit preserves

To make the filling, combine the cheeses, sugar, egg yolk, vanilla, and lemon zest in a bowl. Mix with a wire whisk or fork until light and fluffy. Reserve.

To make the crêpes, sift the flour and salt together into a small mixing bowl.

In a separate bowl, whisk together the water and eggs, then stir the mixture into the flour to make a thin batter.

Grease a griddle or 7-inch skillet with some of the butter and heat over medium-high heat until it sizzles. Ladle or pour in about 2 tablespoons batter and tilt the pan to coat the bottom evenly with a thin coating of batter. Cook the crêpe, on one side only, until it begins to curl away from the sides of the pan, about 1 to 2 minutes.

Slide the crêpe onto a plate and repeat until all the batter is used up, adding butter to the pan as needed and stacking crêpes as they are cooked. You should have about 12 crêpes.

To assemble the blintzes, place about 2 tablespoons of the cheese filling on the center of the uncooked side of each crêpe. Fold in the sides to form small square packets.

Melt 2 to 3 tablespoons of the remaining butter in a skillet over medium-high heat. Place 3 to 4 blintzes in the pan, seam side down, and sauté, turning once, until golden brown on both sides, about 2 to 3 minutes in all. Serve the blintzes at once, topped with sour cream or crème fraîche and your favorite preserves.

Makes 12 blintzes; serves 4.

Cheese Soufflé

To save time, this soufflé can be prepared ahead, frozen, then baked in the morning. Make it with any one of your favorite cheeses or a compatible combination, adding favorite fresh or dried herbs, sautéed minced mushrooms, or finely crumbled cooked bacon if desired. Be sure everyone is seated at the table before the soufflé is done.

1/4 cup (1/2 stick) unsalted butter
1/4 cup unbleached all-purpose flour
1/2 teaspoon salt
1/4 teaspoon freshly grated nutmeg
Freshly ground black pepper
Cayenne pepper
1 1/2 cups low-fat milk
1 1/2 cups shredded cheese (about 6 ounces)
6 eggs, separated
2 egg whites
1/2 teaspoon cream of tartar   *(continued)*

Melt the butter in a medium-sized saucepan over medium-high heat. Using a wire whisk, stir in the flour, salt, nutmeg, and peppers to taste, and whisk until smooth. Add the milk, whisking until smooth, and cook until thick and smooth, about 10 minutes. Add the cheese and stir until it melts and the mixture is smooth. Remove from the heat and beat in the egg yolks, one at a time.

Preheat the oven to 350° F.

Combine all the egg whites in a large bowl and beat until frothy. Add the cream of tartar and continue beating until small peaks form. Using a rubber spatula, fold about half of the whites into the cheese mixture. Gently fold in the remaining whites. Pour into a buttered 2-quart soufflé dish. (Or distribute the mixture into 6 individual 10-ounce soufflé dishes.)

(At this point the soufflé may be placed in the freezer, uncovered, until frozen solid, then well wrapped with foil and frozen for several weeks. Do not thaw before baking; just remove the foil and proceed as follows.)

Fold sheets of foil or baking parchment to form a collar around the top of the soufflé dish to prevent soufflé from running over. Butter the inside of the collar and crimp ends to hold the collar in place. Bake until soufflé is well browned and the top crust feels firm when gently tapped, about 35 to 40 minutes. Do not open the door until the soufflé is almost done. Remove the collar and serve immediately.

Serves 6.

Ricotta Cheese Torta

Flaky phyllo dough encases a slightly sweet cheese filling in this dish, which should be eaten with orange slices or peeled orange segments.

8 ounces cream cheese, softened
3 egg yolks

2 cups ricotta cheese
1/3 cup granulated sugar
1/4 teaspoon salt
3 tablespoons grated orange zest
2 teaspoons vanilla extract
10 sheets (about 1/2 pound) phyllo pastry, thawed (in the refrigerator) if frozen
About 1/2 cup (1 stick) unsalted butter, melted and cooled
Powdered sugar for dusting

In a medium-sized bowl, beat the cream cheese with an electric mixer until fluffy. Add the egg yolks and beat until smooth. Stir in the ricotta, sugar, salt, orange zest, and vanilla until just combined.

Preheat the oven to 400° F.

Place 1 sheet of phyllo on a flat work surface. Keep the remaining dough covered with a lightly dampened towel to prevent it from drying out. With a wide pastry brush, lightly brush the sheet with cooled melted butter to completely cover. Top that phyllo sheet with a second sheet placed at a 45-degree angle to the first sheet and lightly brush it with butter. Repeat until all sheets are used and the sheets form a rough circle of dough. Spoon the cheese mixture onto the center of the top sheet to form a circle about 8 inches in diameter. Bring one side of the phyllo up and over to cover the cheese and brush the top of the dough with butter. Bring the remaining phyllo sides up and over the cheese, overlapping and buttering them as you go, until all sides of the phyllo have been folded over the cheese. Place the phyllo package, seam side down, on a baking sheet and brush the top with melted butter. Bake immediately, or refrigerate as long as overnight.

Bake until the phyllo is golden brown, about 15 minutes. Remove from the oven, dust lightly with powdered sugar, and serve immediately.

Serves 6.

Soft-Cooked Eggs

I first came to enjoy soft-cooked eggs in Holland, where they star at almost every breakfast, along with sliced cold cuts, assorted cheeses, and breads.

6 eggs, at room temperature

Place the eggs in a saucepan and add just enough water to cover. Remove the eggs and bring the water just to a simmer over medium heat. Carefully lower the eggs into the water and simmer, uncovered, until the eggs are done to your taste, 3 to 5 minutes. Drain, and serve the eggs in egg cups. Crack the top gently with a knife and peel away about 1/2 inch of the shell; eat with a spoon. (Or, the eggs can be cracked, peeled, and served in small bowls.)

Serves 3 to 6.

VARIATIONS: Top the cracked eggs with dollops of caviar, sour cream and minced chives, or sautéed crab or tiny shrimp.

Hard-Cooked Eggs

Don't call them "boiled" eggs, because boiling ruins eggs by turning the insides rubbery and cracking the shells, which then leak and create watery eggs.

6 eggs, at room temperature

Place the eggs in a single uncrowded layer in a saucepan. Add just enough water to cover the eggs, place over high heat, and bring to a simmer. Just as soon as the water begins to simmer, reduce the heat to medium and cook for 15 to 18 minutes. Remove from the heat, drain the eggs, and cover immediately with cold water to halt the cooking. Tap each egg all over to crack the shell, then place under running cold water and peel off the shell.

Serves 3 to 6.

Scrambled Eggs

Basic to so many breakfasts, scrambled eggs can be wonderful when properly cooked or rubbery when overcooked.

6 eggs
2 tablespoons milk or heavy (whipping) cream
1/2 teaspoon salt, or to taste
1 1/2 tablespoons unsalted butter
Freshly ground black pepper

Break the eggs into a bowl, add the milk and salt, and beat with a wire whisk or fork until well blended but not frothy.

Heat the butter in a skillet over medium-low heat just until foaming stops. Pour in the eggs. When they begin to set, stir them with a wooden spatula, lifting the edges to let uncooked egg pour underneath. Cook the eggs just until they are almost set but still creamy. Remove immediately to a heated dish and serve. Pass pepper at the table.

Serves 2 or 3.

VARIATIONS: Cook onions, shallots, garlic, mushrooms, sweet peppers, ham, or other meat in the butter before adding the eggs. Or add crumbled cooked bacon, grated cheese, toasted sunflower seeds, minced fresh herbs, or slivered truffles when the eggs are almost set. Top plain scrambled eggs with caviar or smoked salmon.

Sweet Pepper and Onion Frittata

Open-faced Italian omelets are cooked over very low heat until set. Serve piping hot or at room temperature.

For a showy presentation, instead of flipping the frittata in the pan, when the top is about half done, make indentations with a spoon and break quail eggs into the indentations. When almost set, finish under the broiler as directed.

1/4 cup plus 2 tablespoons olive oil
2 cups thinly sliced onion
1 1/2 cups julienned red sweet pepper
2 or 3 garlic cloves, minced or pressed
1/4 cup chopped fresh basil
8 eggs
3 tablespoons light cream (or half-and-half)
1/3 cup freshly grated Parmesan cheese
1/2 teaspoon salt, or to taste
Freshly ground black pepper
2 tablespoons unsalted butter

Heat 1/4 cup of the olive oil in a large heavy skillet over low heat. Add the onion and sweet pepper and cook until vegetables are quite tender and slightly caramelized, about 35 to 45 minutes. Stir in the garlic and basil. Remove from heat and reserve. (This can be done the day before, refrigerated, and reheated in the morning.)

In a bowl, beat the eggs with the light cream, cheese, salt, and black pepper to taste. Reserve.

Over medium heat, melt 1 tablespoon of the butter and 1 tablespoon of the remaining oil in a 12-inch nonstick skillet. Distribute the onion and pepper mixture evenly in the bottom of the skillet. Pour the egg and cheese mixture over the vegetables. Turn the heat to very low and cook the omelet until the eggs are set around the edges. Then gently lift the edges of the omelet with a spatula and tilt the pan to let the uncooked egg run underneath. Continue cooking until the eggs have almost set on top. Place a plate over the top of the pan and invert, turning the frittata onto the plate. Add the remaining 1 tablespoon of butter and oil to the pan and slide the frittata back into the pan, cooked side up. Cook until the bottom is set, 2 to 3 minutes. (Or, do not turn the frittata; cook the almost set omelet under a preheated broiler just until the top is set, about 30 seconds.)

Loosen the edges of the frittata with a spatula and slide it out onto the plate. (Or, place a preheated serving plate over the pan, invert, and turn the frittata out onto the plate.) Cut into wedges to serve.

Serves 4.

Omelets

Once you've mastered the technique, omelets are a quick yet elegant breakfast presentation. If there's a crowd, cook at the table over a portable electric burner. Omelets may be served plain, or with fillings, or topped with a sauce, such as fresh tomato or cheese.

3 eggs
Salt
Freshly ground black or white pepper
1 tablespoon clarified butter (see note)
Filling

In a small bowl, beat the eggs well, then add salt and pepper to taste.

Heat an omelet pan over high heat. Add the clarified butter and heat until very hot but not smoking. Add the eggs and move the pan continuously over the heat to prevent sticking, using a thin spatula to keep eggs away from the sides of the pan. When the bottom sets up, use the spatula to lift up the sides and let any uncooked egg flow underneath. Just before the top is set, add about 1/3 cup filling down the center of the omelet if you wish. Tilting the pan and using the spatula, roll one third of the omelet over the filling. Hold the pan over the serving plate so the unfolded side begins to slide out. Using the spatula, flip omelet so the folded side folds over with the center on the top. Total cooking time should be less than 1 minute. Add a compatible sauce if you wish, and a garnish appropriate to the filling.

Makes 1 omelet; serves 1.

NOTE: To clarify butter, melt 1 cup (2 sticks) butter in a small saucepan over low heat. Remove from the heat and let cool for a few minutes, while milk solids settle to the bottom of the pan. Skim the butterfat from the top and strain the clear (clarified) butter into a container; discard the milk solids. Keeps indefinitely in the refrigerator.

FILLINGS FOR OMELETS

Caviar and sour cream.

Steamed or sautéed vegetables.

Grated cheese, one kind or a combination.

Crumbled crisply cooked bacon.

Cooked and shredded chicken, beef, or pork.

Cooked lobster, shrimp, or crab.

Smoked salmon, sour cream, and minced chives.

Jams or jellies.

Creamed spinach.

Sautéed mushrooms.

Mexican salsa, mild or hot.

Avocado slices.

Baked or Shirred Eggs

6 eggs
Salt
Freshly ground black pepper or ground cayenne
**   pepper**
2 tablespoons unsalted butter, melted
Minced fresh thyme, parsley, or basil, or red sweet
**   pepper cut into julienne, for garnish**

Preheat the oven to 350° F.

Break each egg into a buttered ramekin or other small baking dish. Season to taste with salt and pepper, then cover each egg with 1 teaspoon of the melted butter. Place the dishes in a pan of hot water, cover loosely with sheets of baking parchment, and bake just until the eggs are almost set, about 6 minutes. (The heat from the dish will continue to cook the eggs, so don't overcook in the oven.) Garnish with minced herbs or red pepper strips.

Serves 4.

Eggs with Mild Green Chili Sauce

GREEN CHILI SAUCE

About 12 fresh *tomatillos* (Mexican husk tomatoes),
   or 1 can (13 ounces) *tomatillos*
2 tablespoons vegetable oil
1 cup chopped onion
3 or 4 fresh Anaheim or other mild green chili peppers,
   or 1 can (7 ounces) chopped mild green chili
   peppers
1 to 2 teaspoons minced or pressed garlic
1 tablespoon minced fresh oregano, or 1 teaspoon dried
   oregano leaves (not ground), finely crumbled
1 tablespoon freshly squeezed lime or lemon juice
1/2 teaspoon granulated sugar, or to taste
Salt
1 cup homemade chicken stock or canned low-sodium
   broth
1 bay leaf

Vegetable oil for frying
8 corn tortillas
8 eggs
3 cups cooked shredded chicken, beef, or pork,
   warmed (optional)
2 cups shredded Cheddar or Monterey Jack cheese
   (about 8 ounces), or a combination
Avocado slices or guacamole (use a favorite recipe)
   for garnish
Fresh cilantro (coriander) leaves for garnish

To make the chili sauce, first prepare the *tomatillos*. If using fresh *tomatillos,* remove and discard husks and stems, place in a saucepan, cover with water, and bring to a boil over medium-high heat. Cook until translucent and almost tender, about 5 minutes. Drain, rinse, and drain again. Reserve. If using canned *tomatillos,* drain and reserve.

Heat the oil in a skillet over medium-high heat, add the onion, and cook until soft, about 5 minutes. Transfer to a food processor or blender and add the reserved *tomatillos,* chilies, garlic, oregano, lime juice, sugar, salt to taste, and 1/2 cup of the chicken stock. Blend until smooth.

Transfer the *tomatillo* mixture to a saucepan and add the remaining 1/2 cup chicken stock and the bay leaf. Bring to a boil over medium-high heat, reduce the heat to low, cover, and simmer the sauce until it is slightly thickened and the flavors are well blended, about 30 minutes. Discard the bay leaf. Use the sauce immediately or refrigerate as long as overnight. Reheat before using.

Preheat the oven to 200° F.

Pour oil in a skillet to a depth of 1/2 inch and heat over medium heat. Fry tortillas, one at a time, until crisp and golden. Drain on paper towels and keep warm in the oven.

Retain about 4 tablespoons of the oil in the skillet; discard the rest. Heat the oil over medium heat. Carefully break the eggs into the pan, reduce the heat to medium-low, and cook, basting occasionally with the oil, until done to preference.

Arrange 2 fried tortillas on each of 4 warmed plates. Add some of the Green Chili Sauce, then top with some of the chicken or other meat if desired. Top each tortilla with a fried egg. Drizzle with more hot Green Chili Sauce, sprinkle with cheese, and garnish with avocado and cilantro. Serve immediately.

Serves 4.

Baked Eggs with Creamed Spinach

Around The Rockpile, we still call this old favorite of my partners Eggs Florentine, dating back to the time when just about everything with spinach was termed "Florentine." For a heartier dish, stir about 2 cups chopped cooked chicken or baked ham into the creamed spinach before adding the eggs.

**4 pounds spinach, trimmed, or 2 packages (10 ounces
    each) frozen chopped spinach
1 small package (3 ounces) cream cheese, softened
Salt
Freshly ground black pepper
4 eggs
2 cups grated Cheddar cheese (about 6 ounces)**

Wash the fresh spinach thoroughly and place in a pot with whatever washing water clings to the leaves. Cover, and cook over medium-high heat until tender, about 3 to 5 minutes. Drain well in a sieve, pressing firmly against the spinach to remove all liquid. Coarsely chop the spinach with a knife. If using thawed frozen spinach, squeeze out as much liquid as possible.

Preheat the oven to 375° F.

Combine the spinach and cream cheese in a food processor or blender and purée until well blended but not too smooth. Add salt and pepper to taste. Distribute the creamed spinach among 4 individual buttered ramekins or other ovenproof serving dishes. Make a slight indentation in the center of each and carefully break 1 egg into each indentation. Cover the tops with the grated cheese. Bake, uncovered, until the eggs are set and the cheese is melted and crusty, about 20 minutes.

Serves 4.

Egyptian Twice-Cooked Eggs

Robie Amer of Chico, California, shared this ultra-rich recipe gleaned from her years in Egypt.

**2 tablespoons sesame seeds
3/4 teaspoon ground cumin
1/4 teaspoon freshly grated nutmeg
1/4 teaspoon ground coriander
Salt
Freshly ground black pepper
3/4 cup (1 1/2 sticks) unsalted butter
12 hard-cooked eggs, peeled and sliced lengthwise
    in half
6 small pita breads, warmed and cut horizontally
    in half**

Place the sesame seeds in a small skillet over medium heat, and toast seeds, stirring or shaking the pan, until golden, about 5 minutes. Empty onto a plate to cool.

Combine the cumin, nutmeg, coriander, and salt and pepper to taste in a small bowl and set aside.

Melt the butter in a skillet over low heat until frothy. Add the eggs, cut side down, and cook until the eggs begin to brown, 5 to 6 minutes. Turn the eggs and cook, turning and basting occasionally with the butter in the skillet, until browned on all sides, about 5 minutes more. While the eggs are cooking, sprinkle them with the spice mixture.

To serve, place 2 warm pita bread halves on each plate, then top each half with 2 fried egg halves. Drizzle the seasoned butter from the skillet over the eggs and serve immediately.

Serves 6.

Bacon and Eggs Casserole

Here's a new twist on traditional breakfast fare.

1/2 cup (1 stick) butter
8 ounces fresh mushrooms, preferably wild varieties
    such as *chanterelles,* morels, or *shiitakes,* sliced
1/2 pound thick-sliced bacon, preferably pepper-
    cured, diced
1/2 cup unbleached all-purpose flour
Salt
Freshly ground black pepper
1 quart milk
12 eggs, lightly beaten
3/4 cup light cream (or half-and-half)
1/4 teaspoon salt, or to taste
Fresh chives for garnish

Preheat the oven to 350° F.

Place 2 tablespoons of the butter in a sauté pan or skillet over medium-high heat. Add the mushrooms and cook until lightly browned, about 3 minutes. Reserve.

Fry the bacon in a skillet. Drain the bacon on paper towels and discard the fat from the skillet. To the skillet add 4 tablespoons of the remaining butter, most of the reserved bacon (save some for garnishing), and about three quarters of the mushrooms. Mix well and sprinkle with the flour and salt and black pepper to taste. Gradually stir in the milk and cook, stirring constantly, until the mixture is smooth and thickened, about 20 minutes. Cover and set aside.

Combine the eggs with the light cream and 1/4 teaspoon salt, and cook in the remaining 2 tablespoons butter in a skillet over medium-low heat until very softly scrambled; do not overcook.

In a buttered 9-inch glass soufflé dish, alternately layer the scrambled eggs and the bacon white sauce, ending with sauce. Top with the remaining mushrooms and reserved bacon, then bake, uncovered, until heated through, 15 to 20 minutes. Garnish with chives.

Serves 8.

Scrambled Eggs with Bacon and Vegetables (*Lob Scouse*)

German *lob scouse* is a hearty rendition of bacon and eggs.

1/2 pound bacon, cut into small pieces
1 cup chopped onion
1/2 cup chopped green sweet pepper
3 cups diced cooked potatoes, preferably new potatoes
6 to 8 eggs
Salt
Freshly ground black pepper

Cook the bacon in a large skillet over medium heat until transparent, then add the onion and sweet pepper and cook until soft, about 5 minutes. Add the cooked potatoes and continue cooking until heated through.

Beat the eggs in a bowl, pour into the bacon mixture, and cook, stirring to scramble, until just set. Add salt and pepper to taste. Serve immediately.

Serves 6.

Poached Eggs with Hollandaise Sauce

Rich hollandaise-covered eggs are combined with a variety of other ingredients to create some of America's favorite fancy breakfast dishes. For a change of pace, prepare the sauce with orange juice instead of lemon, or a combination of both juices.

HOLLANDAISE SAUCE
1 cup (2 sticks) unsalted butter
4 egg yolks
3 tablespoons freshly squeezed lemon or orange juice
Cayenne pepper

POACHED EGGS
1 tablespoon white wine vinegar
8 eggs, at room temperature

To make the sauce, cut the butter into 6 to 8 pieces about the same size. In the top of a double boiler over water that is simmering but not boiling, place egg yolks, lemon or orange juice, and 2 pieces of butter. Stir rapidly with a wire whisk until butter melts. Add the remaining pieces of butter, one at a time, stirring until each melts before adding the next piece. When all the butter has been added, stir in a pinch of cayenne. Keep warm over warm water until ready to serve. If the sauce gets too thick or begins to curdle before serving, briskly stir in a small amount of boiling water until smooth.

To poach the eggs, place water in a skillet or shallow pan to a depth of about 2 1/2 inches. Add the vinegar and bring to a boil over medium-high heat. Reduce heat so that the water barely bubbles. Break the eggs one at a time into a cup or small bowl. Using the tip of a slotted spoon, swirl a section of the water to form a small whirlpool. Gently slip the egg into the center of the whirlpool. Repeat with the remaining eggs. Reduce the heat to low and let the eggs steep in hot water until the whites are set, about 3 minutes. Remove eggs from water with a slotted spoon. Drain well and serve at once.

(To poach eggs in quantity, cook as above, then immerse immediately in a bowl of cold water. Refrigerate, covered, up to overnight. To reheat eggs, place them in a bowl of water that is just hot to the touch. Let stand until centers are warm, about 6 to 8 minutes.)

Makes 8 eggs and about 2 cups of sauce; serves 4 to 8.

EGGS BENEDICT: Toast and butter 8 rounds of Holland rusk or English muffin halves. Cover each round with a slice of broiled ham or Canadian bacon. Top with a poached egg, then cover with Hollandaise Sauce.

EGGS BLACKSTONE: Toast and butter 8 English muffin halves. Top each with a slice of broiled tomato, crumbled fried bacon, and a poached egg. Cover with Hollandaise Sauce and garnish with a bit of crumbled bacon.

EGGS SARDOU: Place 1 or 2 cooked large artichoke bottoms on each plate. Top each bottom with a little warm creamed spinach, then a poached egg. Cover with Hollandaise Sauce.

EGGS WITH SALMON: Fill 8 freshly baked puff pastry shells with slivered smoked salmon, top with a poached egg, and cover with Hollandaise Sauce. Garnish with additional salmon and fresh caviar.

EGGS ON SCONES: Split 4 warm Whole Wheat Scones (page 31), top with slices of fried Country Ham (page 83), and then place a poached egg on each. Cover with Hollandaise Sauce made with orange juice and garnish with thin strips of orange zest.

EGGS ST. CHARLES: Top 4 pan-fried rainbow trout with 2 poached eggs and cover with Hollandaise Sauce.

Eggs Hidden in Cheese Sauce and Spinach

Old friend Stephen Marcus introduced this dish to me. It is traditionally made with heavy cream and butter, but Stephen and I prefer this lighter version.

4 pounds spinach, trimmed, or 2 boxes (10 ounces *each*)
     frozen spinach, thawed
5 tablespoons vegetable oil
1 1/2 cups chopped onion
2 tablespoons unbleached all-purpose flour
2 cups low-fat milk or light cream (or half-and-half)
2 cups shredded Monterey Jack cheese (about 8 ounces)
1 teaspoon crushed dried thyme
Salt
Freshly ground white pepper
6 eggs
1 cup shredded Cheddar cheese (about 4 ounces)
Paprika
3 English muffins, split and toasted (optional)

Wash the fresh spinach thoroughly and place in a pot with whatever washing water clings to the leaves. Cover, and cook over medium-high heat until tender, about 3 to 5 minutes. Drain well in a sieve, pressing firmly against the spinach to remove all liquid. If using thawed frozen spinach, squeeze out as much liquid as possible. Coarsely chop the spinach with a knife, and reserve.

Heat 3 tablespoons of the oil in a sauté pan or skillet over medium-high heat. Add the onion and cook, stirring frequently, until onion is soft, about 5 minutes. Stir in the spinach and cook until heated through, about 3 minutes. Reserve.

To make the white sauce, heat the remaining 2 tablespoons oil in a saucepan over medium heat, add the flour, and stir until bubbly, about 3 minutes. Add the milk slowly and stir briskly with a wire whisk or wooden spoon until thick and smooth, about 5 minutes. Add the Jack cheese, thyme, and salt and white pepper to taste; stir until the cheese is melted and the sauce is smooth, about 5 minutes.

Preheat the oven to 350° F.

Place the spinach and onion mixture in a lightly greased ovenproof dish, then cover the spinach with the cheese sauce. Using a large spoon, form 6 evenly spaced wells in the sauce. Break an egg into each well. Cover the top of the casserole with the Cheddar cheese. Sprinkle the top of each egg location heavily with paprika (to aid in serving after baking). Bake until the eggs are set and the cheese is melted, about 20 minutes.

To serve, spoon each section containing an egg onto a toasted English muffin, if desired, or onto 6 individual plates.

Serves 6.

VARIATIONS: For a southwestern flavor, add chopped fresh or canned mild or hot chili peppers to the spinach and onion mixture, and substitute ground chili powder for the paprika. Serve on warm tortillas instead of English muffins.

Create an Italian version by adding minced or pressed garlic to taste to the spinach and onion mixture. Use fresh or dried basil instead of thyme, and substitute Fontina for the Jack cheese and Mozzarella or Parmesan for the Cheddar. Serve on slices of fried polenta.

For a meaty dish, add a layer of cooked chopped chicken, ground beef, or crumbled sausage in the pan before adding the spinach mixture.

Add slivered smoked salmon to the spinach mixture, substitute fresh or dried dill for the thyme, and top the casserole with sour cream to create an elegant version.

Meat, Fish, & Poultry

Country Ham

American country-cured hams are quite strong flavored, a far cry from the water-injected, overnight-cured hams of the supermarket. Fresh hams are seasoned with salt and pepper, then hung to slowly dry in the fragrant smoke of hickory, oak, apple, and other woods. Next, they're aged for a year or more. As they dry and shrink, they achieve the intense flavor that has rivaled prosciutto and other fine European specialty hams in quality, taste, and reputation for 300 years. In times when demand was less intense, hams often aged or cured for as long as seven years, ending up coated with black mold.

Aged hams must be soaked, then thoroughly scrubbed and rinsed off before being boiled or steamed. Next the skin is removed and the hams are baked, with or without a glaze, or sliced and pan fried.

**1 10- to 12-pound country-cured ham,
    aged 4 to 12 months**

Place the ham in a deep container, cover with cold water, and soak: overnight for hams that have aged less than 6 months; 2 to 3 days for hams that have aged from 6 to 12 months. Discard soaking water.

Preheat the oven to 500° F.

With a stiff brush under running cold water, vigorously scrub the ham to remove any dust or mold as well as the pepper coating. Place in a turkey roaster or other container with a tight-fitting cover, add about 6 cups water, cover, and place in the preheated oven for 20 minutes. Then turn off the heat, leaving the ham in the closed oven for about 3 hours.

Turn the oven on again to 500° F. for 15 minutes, then turn off the heat, leaving the ham in the oven for another 3 hours or as long as overnight.

Remove the ham from the pan and trim off the rind with a sharp knife. Slice and eat as is, or store in the refrigerator and slice and fry whenever you wish. Serve with red-eye gravy, grits, and biscuits. (Or, cover the baked and trimmed ham a favorite glaze and cook in a 375° F. oven, basting occasionally with the drippings, until the glaze is set and browned, about 20 minutes.)

Serves 20.

Fried Ham with Red-Eye Gravy

Gravy made from the frying drippings is dubbed "red eye" after the pool of grease that forms in the center of the skillet. Sometimes a bit of coffee is added to darken the gravy before it is served over grits or hot biscuits.

**4 1/4-inch slices country ham
1 cup water
1 or 2 tablespoons black coffee (optional)
Cooked grits**

Place the ham slices in a heavy skillet over low heat and cook until tender and lightly browned, about 20 minutes. Remove the ham to a warm plate. Add about 1 cup water to the skillet and cook, stirring to loosen all the browned bits. Boil about 2 minutes, adding coffee if desired to darken the gravy. Serve the gravy over the ham and grits.

Serves 4.

Scrapple

Originally, leftover parts of pork, including necks, shoulders, and feet, went into this Pennsylvania Dutch breakfast dish. This simple version that relies on good pork sausage was shared by Barbara Fritz. It's a special favorite of her father, Emanuel. Since helping to decorate for his 100th birthday celebration, I've wondered if eating scrapple for breakfast contributes to longevity in spite of the high cholesterol content.

1 pound bulk pork sausage, mild or hot
5 cups water
1 1/2 cups yellow cornmeal
1 teaspoon crumbled dried sage leaves
1 teaspoon dried marjoram
1/2 teaspoon dried thyme
Salt
Freshly ground black pepper
About 1/2 cup (1 stick) butter for frying
Maple syrup, warmed (optional)

Break up the sausage and add it to the water in a large stockpot over high heat. Bring to a boil, then reduce heat so the water is at a simmer. While stirring continuously with a long-handled wooden spoon, add the cornmeal in a slow, steady stream. Add the sage, marjoram, thyme, and salt and pepper to taste. Simmer, stirring quite frequently, until thickened, about 15 minutes. Cover, and simmer until very thick, about 1 hour.

Pour the mixture into a lightly greased 9 x 5-inch loaf pan, pressing it evenly into the corners. Cover with plastic wrap and refrigerate overnight or up to 3 days.

To remove the scrapple loaf, briefly dip the pan into hot water and slide a blunt knife around the edges.

Invert the scrapple onto a flat surface and remove the pan. Slice the loaf as you would bread.

Preheat the oven to 200° F.

In a large skillet over medium-high heat, melt the butter, about 2 tablespoons at a time as needed, until foamy. Add a few scrapple slices at a time and fry until golden brown on one side, about 8 to 10 minutes. Turn and brown the other side, about 8 to 10 minutes more. Transfer to an ovenproof dish and keep warm in the oven until all the slices are cooked, adding the remaining butter as needed. Serve warm, with warmed maple syrup if desired.

Serves 6 to 8.

Pan-Fried Pork Tenderloin

For a change of pace from bacon, ham, or sausage, serve this fresh pork dish with warmed chunky applesauce, or apple slices sautéed with onion.

1 pork tenderloin, sliced 1/2 inch thick
Salt
Freshly ground black pepper
Flour for dredging
1/2 cup (1 stick) butter

Season the pork slices with salt and pepper to taste, then dredge in flour. Heat the butter in a skillet over medium-high heat, add the pork slices, and cook, turning occasionally, until tender and just past the pink stage inside, about 5 minutes.

Serves 4 to 6.

Apple-Pork Sausage Patties

Store the mixture in the refrigerator, breaking off as much as needed at any one time; use within a week.

1 1/2 pounds ground pork butt, with some fat
1/4 cup unsweetened frozen apple juice concentrate,
    thawed
1/2 teaspoon salt
1/2 teaspoon freshly ground black pepper
1/8 teaspoon ground cayenne pepper
1 teaspoon crumbled dried whole leaf sage
1/2 teaspoon dried thyme, crumbled
1/4 teaspoon ground allspice

In a large bowl, combine the ground pork, apple juice, salt, peppers, sage, thyme, and allspice. Mix well, using your hands if necessary to blend spices into meat. Break off a bit of the mixture and cook in a hot skillet, then taste. Adjust seasonings to taste. Wrap well and refrigerate for several hours or overnight to blend the flavors.

Break off pieces of the sausage, roll into 1 1/2-inch balls, and flatten.

To cook, add just enough water to barely cover the bottom of a heavy skillet. Add several sausage patties and cook over medium-high heat, turning, until the water evaporates. Reduce the heat to low and cook until the patties are brown and crusty, 10 to 15 minutes. Repeat with remaining patties. Drain on paper towels before serving. (Or, cook on baking sheets in 375° F. oven until browned, 20 to 25 minutes.)

Makes about 24 patties.

Fried Coppa

Coppa is an Italian-style pork product that's usually thinly sliced and eaten cold. Fried, it's a flavorful change of pace from bacon.

1/2 pound thinly sliced coppa

Heat a heavy skillet over medium-high heat, add the coppa, and cook, turning frequently, until the meat is crinkly, about 4 minutes. Drain briefly on paper towels and serve hot.

Serves 4.

Corned Beef Hash

I prefer hash without the traditional crust from overcooking. If you feel differently, cook on one side until brown and crusty, invert, and cook the other side until crusty. Hash and fried catfish are the two dishes I enjoy with tomato catsup.

1 pound unpeeled red potatoes
2 tablespoons vegetable oil
1/4 cup (1/2 stick) butter
1 large onion, sliced
2 medium red sweet peppers, cut into julienne
2 or 3 garlic cloves, minced or pressed
3 to 4 cups cooked corned beef brisket, thinly sliced,
        then cut into julienne
1 tablespoon fresh thyme, or 1 teaspoon dried thyme
Salt
Freshly ground black pepper or ground cayenne pepper
1 tablespoon Worcestershire sauce, or to taste
1/2 cup chopped parsley, preferably flat-leaf
        Italian type
4 to 6 poached eggs (page 78)
Fresh parsley or thyme sprigs for garnish

Boil the potatoes until they are tender but still hold together, about 15 minutes. Cool, then slice and cut into julienne.

Heat the oil and 2 tablespoons of the butter in a sauté pan or skillet over medium heat, add the onion and sweet peppers, and cook, stirring occasionally, until vegetables are very soft but not browned, about 20 minutes. Stir in the garlic and cook 1 minute. Add the remaining 2 tablespoons butter, the reserved potatoes, corned beef, thyme, and salt, pepper, and Worcestershire to taste. Cook until the meat and potatoes are heated through, about 8 minutes. Stir in the parsley and distribute among 4 to 6 individual plates. Top with a poached egg and garnish with parsley or thyme sprigs.

Serves 4 to 6.

VARIATION: Substitute shredded cooked chicken for the corned beef.

Joe's Special

Serve this old San Francisco Italian favorite with warmed crusty sourdough bread and good sweet butter.

2 tablespoons olive oil
1 1/2 cups chopped onion
1 1/2 pounds ground beef, crumbled
2 garlic cloves, minced or pressed
1/2 pound mushrooms, sliced
2 pounds coarsely chopped fresh spinach, or 1 package
        (10 ounces) frozen spinach, thawed and
        well drained
1 1/2 teaspoons minced fresh oregano, or
        1/2 teaspoon dried oregano
Salt
Freshly ground black pepper
Freshly grated nutmeg
5 eggs, lightly beaten
Freshly grated Parmesan cheese for passing

Heat the olive oil in a sauté pan or skillet over high heat, add the onion, and cook until soft but not browned, about 5 minutes. Add the ground beef, garlic, and mushrooms, and sauté until the meat is lightly browned, just past the pink stage, about 10 minutes. Add the spinach and cook, stirring, for 5 minutes. Add the oregano and salt, pepper, and nutmeg to taste. Reduce the heat to low and add the eggs, stirring until the eggs are just set but still soft. Serve immediately, and pass the cheese for sprinkling over the top.

Serves 6.

Grillades and Grits

Old Creole New Orleans gave America this special breakfast dish of braised veal, which is always accompanied by grits to soak up the rich gravy. Lard is still used for sautéing the veal in most New Orleans kitchens, but I prefer a mixture of vegetable oil and butter.

**6 5- to 6-ounce boneless veal round steaks,
    about 1/2 inch thick**
Salt
Freshly ground black pepper
Ground cayenne pepper
Flour for dredging
3 tablespoons vegetable oil
3 tablespoons unsalted butter
2 1/2 cups chopped onion
1 1/2 tablespoons minced or pressed garlic
**2 cups coarsely chopped ripe tomatoes or canned
    Italian-style plum tomatoes, drained**
**2 cups homemade veal or chicken stock or canned
    low-sodium chicken broth**
1 bay leaf
1 1/2 cups grits, cooked according to package directions

Trim away all fat from the veal and cut the meat into pieces 2 to 3 inches in diameter. Place the meat between 2 sheets of waxed paper and pound with a mallet or other flat instrument to a thickness of about 1/8 inch. Season to taste with salt and peppers. Dip the meat into the flour to coat lightly, shaking off excess flour.

In a sauté pan or skillet, heat 1 tablespoon of the vegetable oil and 1 tablespoon of the butter over medium heat. Add the veal pieces a few at a time and brown on both sides. Transfer to a platter as they are browned; reserve.

Add the remaining oil and butter and cook the onion until soft but not browned, about 5 minutes. Stir in the garlic and cook 1 minute. Add the tomato, stock, and

bay leaf. Bring to a boil over high heat, then partially cover, reduce the heat to low, and simmer for 20 minutes.

Add the reserved veal and simmer, partially covered, turning the veal every 10 minutes to coat with the gravy, until the meat is tender when pierced with a sharp knife, about 30 minutes. Remove the meat to a heated platter and keep warm.

Reheat the gravy just before serving. Mound the cooked grits on heated individual plates, add the veal grillades, cover both with the gravy, and serve immediately.

Serves 6.

Breakfast Steaks

Serve with Brabant Potatoes (page 92) and baked, fried, or poached eggs.

Salt
Freshly ground black pepper
4 3-ounce slices beef fillet
1/4 cup Worcestershire sauce
2 tablespoons butter
Juice of 1 lemon

Heat a skillet over high heat until very hot. Salt and pepper the fillets on both sides to taste, pressing the seasoning in with your fingers. Place the steaks in the hot pan and immediately reduce the heat to low. Sear briefly on one side, about 45 seconds, turn the steaks, and sear the other side. Continue cooking, turning occasionally, until the steaks are done to your taste, 5 to 15 minutes. While the steaks are cooking, sprinkle with the Worcestershire sauce, top each with butter, and add the lemon juice. Serve the steaks immediately, drizzling with any pan juices that are left.

Serves 4.

Smoked Fish with Rice (Kedgeree)

Anglo-Indian in origin, *kedgeree* is traditionally made with finnan haddie (smoked haddock). I dislike the strong smell and flavor, and prefer the dish made with smoked trout, sablefish, or whitefish.

1/2 pound smoked fish, flaked
2 cups cooked long-grain brown or white rice
1/4 pound smoked ham, cut into julienne
1/2 cup chopped fresh parsley
1/4 cup (1/2 stick) unsalted butter, melted
1/4 cup heavy (whipping) cream or light cream
    (or half-and-half)
Salt
Ground cayenne pepper
3 hard-cooked eggs, sliced or grated
Fresh parsley leaflets, preferably flat-leaf Italian type,
    for garnish

Preheat the oven to 350° F.

Combine the flaked fish, rice, ham, parsley, melted butter, cream, and salt and cayenne pepper to taste in a large bowl. Toss thoroughly and pour into a buttered ovenproof dish. Arrange the eggs on top, cover tightly with a fitted cover or foil, and bake until hot, about 20 minutes. Garnish with parsley before serving.

Serves 4 to 6.

Pan-Fried Fish

Although trout is the most popular breakfast fish, almost any fish makes a tasty addition to the breakfast table. In addition to this method, try grilling, steaming, or poaching your favorite fish. Be sure the fish is very fresh, and avoid overcooking; fish is done when the flesh just turns opaque.

4 10- to 12-ounce fresh rainbow trout or other small whole
    fish, boned, or 4 6- to 8-ounce fish steaks or fillets
Salt
Freshly ground black pepper
Flour for dredging
Vegetable oil for pan frying
Butter for pan frying
1/2 cup (1 stick) unsalted butter
3 tablespoons freshly squeezed lemon juice
1/4 cup minced fresh parsley, preferably flat-leaf
    Italian type
Thinly sliced lemon for garnish
Fresh parsley sprigs for garnish

Clean the whole fish, leaving the heads and tails intact. Split the fish and remove the backbone, then fold back into shape. Wash fish in cold water and pat dry with paper towels. Season with salt and pepper and dredge in flour.

Combine equal parts oil and butter to a depth of 1/4 inch in the bottom of a skillet large enough to hold the fish. Heat over medium-high heat until the butter is foamy, add the fish, and cook, turning, until golden brown on both sides. Remove the fish to heated plates and discard the cooking fat.

Wipe out the skillet with paper towels, place over medium-high heat, add the 1/2 cup butter, and cook until the butter is very lightly browned. Stir in the lemon juice and minced parsley and pour over the trout. Garnish with lemon slices and parsley sprigs. Serve hot.

Serves 4.

Braised Quail

For as long as I can remember, my mother has cooked braised quail for Christmas breakfast. I've added my own touches to her recipe. Serve with a fresh fruit compote and hot biscuits with sweet butter and good jam.

4 strips thick-sliced bacon
8 quail, ready to cook
Salt
Freshly ground black pepper
Flour for dredging
1/4 cup (1/2 stick) butter
1/2 pound fresh mushrooms, preferably wild types
     such as *chanterelles,* morels, or *shiitakes,* sliced
1 cup homemade chicken stock or canned low-sodium
     broth
1 tablespoon fresh thyme, or 1 teaspoon dried thyme
1/2 cup heavy (whipping) cream or light cream
     (or half-and-half)
8 pieces Fried Polenta (page 56) or toasted whole wheat
     bread (optional)
Fresh thyme or parsley sprigs for garnish

Fry the bacon in a skillet until crisp. Drain on paper towels, crumble, and reserve.

Season the quail with salt and pepper to taste, then dredge in flour.

In a flameproof casserole that has a tight-fitting cover, heat the butter over medium-high heat, add the birds, and brown on all sides, about 5 minutes. Remove the quail with a slotted spoon or tongs and reserve. Add the mushrooms to the casserole and sauté until tender, about 5 minutes. Add the stock, thyme, and cream; stir to blend well. Return the quail to the casserole, cover tightly, and cook over medium heat, turning the quail frequently, until meat is tender when pierced with a fork, 45 minutes to 1 hour. (Or, place the casserole in a 325° F. oven to cook.) Transfer the quail to a warm platter. Increase the heat under the casserole and stir until the sauce is slightly reduced and thick.

To serve, place quail on fried polenta or toast, if desired, and spoon the sauce over the top. Sprinkle with crumbled bacon and garnish with fresh thyme or parsley sprigs.

Serves 4 to 8.

Brabant Potatoes

This garlicky dish (not named, incidentally, for my photographer) from New Orleans is a hearty accompaniment to meat or egg dishes, and a good change from ubiquitous hash browns.

1/4 cup (1/2 stick) butter
1 teaspoon minced or pressed garlic
4 medium-sized white potatoes
Vegetable oil for frying
2 tablespoons minced fresh parsley
Salt
Ground cayenne pepper

Melt the butter in a small sauté pan or skillet over low heat. Add the garlic and sauté for about 5 minutes. Do not allow the garlic to brown. Strain; reserve the butter and discard the garlic.

Peel the potatoes and cut them into about 1-inch cubes. Place in ice water to crisp, then pat them dry with paper towels.

Heat oil to 320° F. in a deep fryer.

Add the potatoes to the hot oil and fry until soft and pale yellow, about 3 minutes. Remove with a slotted spoon and drain on paper towels.

Increase the temperature of the oil to 375° F. and preheat the oven to 200° F.

Add the drained potatoes to the oil and fry until crisp and golden, about 3 minutes. Remove with a slotted spoon and drain again on paper towels.

Place the well-drained potatoes in a deep bowl and toss them with the reserved garlic butter, the parsley, and salt and cayenne pepper to taste. Transfer to a baking sheet lined with paper towels and place in the oven for about 20 minutes before serving.

Serves 6.

INDEX

Produced by The Rockpile Press, San Francisco
    and Lake Tahoe

Art direction, book design, and styling by
    James McNair
Editorial production assistance by Lin Cotton
Studio kitchen assistance by Gail High
Photographic assistance by Louis Block
Typography and mechanicals by
    Chuck Thayer Associates, San Francisco

Acknowledgments:

To my agent, Martha Casselman, for making the Arbor House connection, loaning props, and providing assistance throughout the project.

To those who shared recipes, sampled recipe testing, gave numerous suggestions, loaned props, and offered encouragement, especially Robie Amer, Ed Broussard, Don Bull, Burke and Joyce Carr, John Carr, Barbara Fritz, Louis Hicks, Ken and Christine High, the Tad Highs, Jim Hildreth, Douglas Jackson, Doris Keith, Mark Leno, Mary McCoy, James and Lucille McNair, Martha McNair, Stephen Marcus, Marian May, Lenny Meyer, Jack Porter, Tom and Nancy Reiss, Marilyn Babs Retzer, John Richardson, Bob and Kristi Spence, Burt Tessler, Jim Wentworth, and Kathryn Wittenmyer.

To Patricia Brabant and her assistant Louis Block for another gorgeous collaboration and for making each photo session seem more like a party than a workday.

To Gail High for managing to keep the studio kitchen functioning during the photography.

To Lee Simmons of Arbor House and Kathie Ness for superb and speedy editorial direction.

To Cleve Gallat and Peter Linato of Chuck Thayer Associates for transforming my text and layouts into typography and beautiful pages.

And to my crew at The Rockpile Press—Lin Cotton, Addie Prey, Buster Booroo, Joshua J. Chew, and Michael T. Wigglebutt—for all their loyal services throughout writing, recipe development and testing, and photography.